MznLnx

Rico Publications

Exam Prep for Vector Calculus
3rd Edition
Colley

Publisher: Raymond Houge
Assistant Editor: Michael Rouger
Text and Cover Designer: Lisa Buckner
Marketing Manager: Sara Swagger
Project Manager, Editorial Production: Jerry Emerson
Art Director: Vernon Lowerui

Product Manager: Dave Mason
Editorial Assitant: Rachel Guzmanji
Pedagogy: Debra Long
Cover Image: Jim Reed/Getty Images
Text and Cover Printer: City Printing, Inc.
Compositor: Media Mix, Inc.

(c) 2010 Rico Publications
ALL RIGHTS RESERVED. No part of this work covered by the copyright may be reproduced or used in any form or by an means--graphic, electronic, or mechanical, including photocopying, recording, taping, Web distribution, information storage, and retrieval systems, or in any other manner--without the written permission of the publisher.

Printed in the United States
ISBN:

For more information about our products, contact us at:
Dave.Mason@RicoPublications.com

For permission to use material from this text or product, submit a request online to:
Dave.Mason@RicoPublications.com

MznLnx

Missing Links Exam Preps

Exam Prep for

Vector Calculus

Colley, 3rd Edition

The MznLnx Exam Prep is your link from the texbook and lecture to your exams.
The MznLnx Exam Preps are unauthorized and comprehensive reviews of your textbooks.

All material provided by MznLnx and Rico Publications (c) 2010
Textbook publishers and textbook authors do not particpate in or contribute to these reviews.

Contents

CHAPTER 1
Vectors — 1

CHAPTER 2
Differentiation in Several Variables — 14

CHAPTER 3
Multiple Integration — 49

CHAPTER 4
Line Integrals — 59

CHAPTER 5
Surface Integrals and Vector Analysis — 67

CHAPTER 6
Vector Analysis in Higher Dimensions — 81

ANSWER KEY — 87

TO THE STUDENT

COMPREHENSIVE

The *MznLnx* Exam Prep series is designed to help you pass your exams. Editors at MznLnx review your textbooks and then prepare these practice exams to help you master the textbook material. Unlike study guides, workbooks, and practice tests provided by the texbook publisher and textbook authors, *MznLnx* gives you **all** of the material in each chapter in exam form, not just samples, so you can be sure to nail your exam.

MECHANICAL

The MznLnx Exam Prep series creates exams that will help you learn the subject matter as well as test you on your understanding. Each question is designed to help you master the concept. Just working through the exams, you gain an understanding of the subject--its a simple mechanical process that produces success.

INTEGRATED STUDY GUIDE AND REVIEW

MznLnx is not just a set of exams designed to test you, its also a comprehensive review of the subject content. Each exam question is also a review of the concept, making sure that you will get the answer correct without having to go to other sources of material. You learn as you go! Its the easiest way to pass an exam.

HUMOR

Studying can be tedious and dry. MznLnx's instructional design includes moderate humor within the exam questions on occassion, to break the tedium and revitalize the brain

Chapter 1. Vectors

1. In mathematics, a _____ is a method for approximating the total area underneath a curve on a graph, otherwise known as an integral. It may also be used to define the integration operation.

Consider a function $f: D \rightarrow \mathbf{R}$, where D is a subset of the real numbers $\mathbf{R}$, and let $I = [a, b]$ be a closed interval contained in D. A finite set of points $\{x_0, x_1, x_2, \ldots x_n\}$ such that $a = x_0 < x_1 < x_2 \ldots < x_n = b$ creates a partition

$$P = \{[x_0, x_1), [x_1, x_2), \ldots [x_{n-1}, x_n]\}$$

of I.

a. Riemann sum
b. Signed measure
c. Risch algorithm
d. Solid of revolution

2. In elementary mathematics, physics, and engineering, a _____ is a geometric object that has both a magnitude (or length), direction and sense, (i.e., orientation along the given direction.) A _____ is frequently represented by a line segment with a definite direction, or graphically as an arrow, connecting an initial point A with a terminal point B, and denoted by

The magnitude of the _____ is the length of the segment and the direction characterizes the displacement of B relative to A: how much one should move the point A to 'carry' it to the point B.

Many algebraic operations on real numbers have close analogues for vectors.

a. BDDC
b. Linear partial differential operator
c. 15 theorem
d. Vector

3. In mathematics, _____ is one of the basic operations defining a vector space in linear algebra Note that _____ is different from scalar product which is an inner product between two vectors.

More specifically, if K is a field and V is a vector space over K, then _____ is a function from K × V to V. The result of applying this function to c in K and v in V is denoted cv.

Chapter 1. Vectors

a. Vector-valued function
b. Scalar multiplication
c. Homogeneous function
d. Direction cosines

4. In geometry, a _____ is a quadrilateral with two sets of parallel sides. The opposite or facing sides of a _____ are of equal length, and the opposite angles of a _____ are of equal size. The three-dimensional counterpart of a _____ is a parallelepiped.
   a. BIBO stability
   b. 15 theorem
   c. BDDC
   d. Parallelogram

5. In physics, displacement is the vector that specifies the change in position of a point or a particle in reference to a previous position. When the previous point is the origin, this is better referred to as a position. _____ versus distance traveled along a path.
   a. 15 theorem
   b. BDDC
   c. BIBO stability
   d. Displacement vector

6. In physics, _____ is movement that changes the position of an object, as opposed to rotation. For example, according to Whittaker:

A _____ is the operation changing the positions of all points (x, y, z) of an object according to the formula

$$(x, y, z) \rightarrow (x + \Delta x, y + \Delta y, z + \Delta z)$$

where $(\Delta x, \Delta y, \Delta z)$ is the same vector for each point of the object. The _____ vector $(\Delta x, \Delta y, \Delta z)$ common to all points of the object describes a particular type of displacement of the object, usually called a linear displacement to distinguish it from displacements involving rotation, called angular displacements.

a. 15 theorem
b. BIBO stability
c. Translation
d. BDDC

Chapter 1. Vectors

7. In vector calculus, the _____ is shorthand for either the _____ matrix or its determinant, the _____ determinant.

In algebraic geometry the _____ of a curve means the _____ variety: a group variety associated to the curve, in which the curve can be embedded.

These concepts are all named after the mathematician Carl Gustav Jacob Jacobi.

a. Saddle surface
b. Vector Laplacian
c. Jacobian
d. Critical point

8. A _____, $F_{net} = F_1 + F_2 + …$ (also known as a resultant force) is a vector produced when two or more forces { F_1, F_2, … } act upon a single object. It is calculated by vector addition of the force vectors acting upon the object. A _____ can also be defined as the overall force acting on an object, when all the individual forces acting on the object are added together.

a. 15 theorem
b. BIBO stability
c. BDDC
d. Net force

9. In mathematics, the _____ of two monic polynomials P and Q over a field k is defined as the product

$$\text{res}(P, Q) = \prod_{(x,y):\, P(x)=0,\, Q(y)=0} (x - y),$$

of the differences of their roots, where x and y take on values in the algebraic closure of k. For non-monic polynomials with leading coefficients p and q, respectively, the above product is multiplied by

$$p^{\deg Q} q^{\deg P}.$$

- The _____ is the determinant of the Sylvester matrix (and of the Bezout matrix.)

- When Q is separable, the above product can be rewritten to

$$\operatorname{res}(P, Q) = \prod_{P(x)=0} Q(x)$$

and this expression remains unchanged if Q is reduced modulo P. Note that, when non-monic, this includes the factor $q^{\deg P}$ but still needs the factor $p^{\deg Q}$.

- Let $P' = P \mod Q$. The above idea can be continued by swapping the roles of P' and Q. However, P' has a set of roots different from that of P. This can be resolved by writing $\prod_{Q(y)=0} P'(y)$ as a determinant again, where P' has leading zero coefficients. This determinant can now be simplified by iterative expansion with respect to the column, where only the leading coefficient q of Q appears.

$$\operatorname{res}(P, Q) = q^{\deg P - \deg P'} \cdot \operatorname{res}(P', Q)$$

Continuing this procedure ends up in a variant of the Euclidean algorithm. This procedure needs quadratic runtime.

a. Leading coefficient
b. Difference polynomial
c. Quadratic function
d. Resultant

10.   In mathematics, _____ are a method of defining a curve. A simple kinematical example is when one uses a time parameter to determine the position, velocity, and other information about a body in motion.

Abstractly, a relation is given in the form of an equation, and it is shown also to be the image of functions from items such as R^n.

a. Partial derivative
b. Shift theorem
c. Critical point
d. Parametric equations

11. In mathematics, _____ and minima, known collectively as extrema, are the largest value (maximum) or smallest value (minimum), that a function takes in a point either within a given neighbourhood (local extremum) or on the function domain in its entirety (global extremum.)

Throughout, a point refers to an input (x), while a value refers to an output (y): one distinguishing between the maximum value and the point (or points) at which it occurs.

A real-valued function f defined on the real line is said to have a local maximum point at the point x^*, if there exists some $\varepsilon > 0$, such that $f(x^*) \geq f(x)$ when $|x - x^*| < \varepsilon$.

a. Racetrack principle
b. Maxima
c. Related rates
d. Leibniz formula

12. A _____ is the curve defined by the path of a point on the edge of circular wheel as the wheel rolls along a straight line. It is an example of a roulette, a curve generated by a curve rolling on another curve.

The _____ is the solution to the brachistochrone problem (i.e. it is the curve of fastest descent under gravity) and the related tautochrone problem (i.e. the period of a ball rolling back and forth inside it does not depend on the ball's starting position.)

a. Curtate cycloid
b. Prolate cycloid
c. Tractrix
d. Cycloid

13. A _____ spheroid is a spheroid in which the polar diameter is greater than the equatorial diameter. A _____ spheroid

The _____ spheroid is the shape of the ball in several sports, such as Rugby Football and Australian Rules Football. American Football and Canadian Football use a pointed _____ spheroid (also resembling a rotated vesica piscis.)

a. Hyperbolic paraboloid
b. Normal vector
c. Parametric surface
d. Prolate

14. A _____ is a statement of the meaning of a word or phrase. The term to be defined is known as the definiendum. The words which define it are known as the definiens.
a. BIBO stability
b. 15 theorem
c. BDDC
d. Definition

15. In mathematics, the _____ is an operation which takes two vectors over the real numbers R and returns a real-valued scalar quantity. It is the standard inner product of the orthonormal Euclidean space. It contrasts with the cross product which produces a vector result.
a. Homogeneous function
b. Vector-valued function
c. Scalar multiplication
d. Dot product

16. In mathematics, an _____ space is a vector space with the additional structure of _____. This additional structure associates each pair of vectors in the space with a scalar quantity known as the _____ of the vectors. Inner products allow the rigorous introduction of intuitive geometrical notions such as the length of a vector or the angle between two vectors.
a. Inner product
b. AUSM
c. ACTRAN
d. ALGOR

17. _____ is the long dimension of any object. The _____ of a thing is the distance between its ends, its linear extent as measured from end to end. This may be distinguished from height, which is vertical extent, and width or breadth, which are the distance from side to side, measuring across the object at right angles to the _____.
a. BDDC
b. Length
c. BIBO stability
d. 15 theorem

Chapter 1. Vectors

18. In mathematics, two vectors are _____ if they are perpendicular, i.e., they form a right angle. For example, a subway and the street above, although they do not physically intersect, are _____ if they cross at a right angle.
    a. ACTRAN
    b. AUSM
    c. ALGOR
    d. Orthogonal

19. In mathematics, a _____ in a normed vector space is a vector (often a spatial vector) whose length is 1 (the unit length.) A _____ is often denoted by a lowercase letter with a superscribed caret or e;hate;, like this: $\hat{i}$.

    In Euclidean space, the dot product of two unit vectors is simply the cosine of the angle between them.

    a. Overdetermined
    b. ALGOR
    c. ACTRAN
    d. Unit vector

20. In mathematics a _____ is a construction in vector calculus which associates a vector to every point in a (locally) Euclidean space.

    Vector fields are often used in physics to model, for example, the speed and direction of a moving fluid throughout space, or the strength and direction of some force, such as the magnetic or gravitational force, as it changes from point to point.

    In the rigorous mathematical treatment, (tangent) vector fields are defined on manifolds as sections of a manifold's tangent bundle.

    a. BDDC
    b. 15 theorem
    c. BIBO stability
    d. Vector field

21. The vector resolute (also known as the _____) of two vectors, $\mathbf{a}$ in the direction of $\mathbf{b}$ (also '$\mathbf{a}$ on $\mathbf{b}$'), is given by:

    $$(\mathbf{a} \cdot \hat{\mathbf{b}})\hat{\mathbf{b}} \text{ or } (|\mathbf{a}|\cos\theta)\hat{\mathbf{b}}$$

    where θ is the angle between the vectors $\mathbf{b}$ and $\mathbf{a}$ and $\hat{\mathbf{b}}$ is the unit vector in the direction of $\mathbf{b}$.

The vector resolute is a vector, and is the orthogonal projection of the vector a onto the vector b. The vector resolute is also said to be a component of vector a in the direction of vector b.

a. BDDC
b. BIBO stability
c. 15 theorem
d. Vector projection

22. In mathematics, the _____ is a binary operation on two vectors in a three-dimensional Euclidean space that results in another vector which is perpendicular to the plane containing the two input vectors. The algebra defined by the _____ is neither commutative nor associative. It contrasts with the dot product which produces a scalar result.

a. Permutation
b. 15 theorem
c. Fundamental theorem of algebra
d. Cross product

23. In mathematics and physics, the _____ is a common mnemonic for understanding notation conventions for vectors in 3 dimensions. It was invented for use in electromagnetism by British physicist Zachariah William Cole in the late 1800s.

When choosing three vectors that must be at right angles to each other, there are two distinct solutions, so when expressing this idea in mathematics, one must remove the ambiguity of which solution is meant.

a. BIBO stability
b. BDDC
c. 15 theorem
d. Right-hand rule

24. In algebra, a _____ is a function depending on n that associates a scalar, det(A), to an n×n square matrix A. The fundamental geometric meaning of a _____ is a scale factor for measure when A is regarded as a linear transformation. Determinants are important both in calculus, where they enter the substitution rule for several variables, and in multilinear algebra.

For a fixed nonnegative integer n, there is a unique _____ function for the n×n matrices over any commutative ring R. In particular, this function exists when R is the field of real or complex numbers.

Chapter 1. Vectors

a. 15 theorem
b. BIBO stability
c. BDDC
d. Determinant

25. In physics (specifically mechanics and electrical engineering), _____ ω (also referred to by the terms angular speed, radial frequency, circular frequency, orbital frequency, and radian frequency) is a scalar measure of rotation rate. _____ is the magnitude of the vector quantity angular velocity. The term _____ vector $\vec{\omega}$ is sometimes used as a synonym for the vector quantity angular velocity .
   a. ACTRAN
   b. Angular frequency
   c. ALGOR
   d. AUSM

26. _____ is the tendency of a force to rotate an object about an axis (or fulcrum or pivot.) Just as a force is a push or a pull, a _____ can be thought of as a twist. The symbol for _____ is τ, the Greek letter tau.
   a. BDDC
   b. 15 theorem
   c. BIBO stability
   d. Torque

27. In mathematics and its applications, a _____ system is a system for assigning an n-tuple of numbers or scalars to each point in an n-dimensional space. This concept is part of the theory of manifolds. 'Scalars' in many cases means real numbers, but, depending on context, can mean complex numbers or elements of some other commutative ring.
   a. Cylindrical coordinate system
   b. Coordinate
   c. Spherical coordinate system
   d. 15 theorem

28. _____ is a term in geometry and in everyday life that refers to a property in Euclidean space of two or more lines or planes, or a combination of these. The existence and properties of parallel lines are the basis of Euclid's parallel postulate. Two lines parallel would be denoted as ABC DEF.
   a. BDDC
   b. 15 theorem
   c. BIBO stability
   d. Parallelism

29. In economics, the _____ functional form of production functions is widely used to represent the relationship of an output to inputs. It was proposed by Knut Wicksell (1851-1926), and tested against statistical evidence by Charles Cobb and Paul Douglas in 1900-1928.

For production, the function is

$$Y = AL^{\alpha}K^{\beta},$$

where:

- Y = total production (the monetary value of all goods produced in a year)
- L = labor input
- K = capital input
- A = total factor productivity
- α and β are the output elasticities of labor and capital, respectively. These values are constants determined by available technology.

Output elasticity measures the responsiveness of output to a change in levels of either labor or capital used in production, ceteris paribus. For example if α = 0.15, a 1% increase in labor would lead to approximately a 0.15% increase in output.

   a. BDDC
   b. 15 theorem
   c. BIBO stability
   d. Cobb-Douglas

30. Someone who is _____ will prefer to use this hand for everyday activities, such as writing, maintaining personal hygiene, cooking and so forth. According to a variety of studies, anywhere from 70% to 90% of the world population is _____, while most of the remaining are left-handed. A small percentage of the population can use both hands equally well; a person with this ability is deemed to be ambidextrous (though such people may still have a personal preference of one hand over the other.)
   a. 15 theorem
   b. Right-handed
   c. BIBO stability
   d. BDDC

31. In computer science and information science, _____ could also be a method or an algorithm. Again, an example will illustrate: There are systems of counting, as with Roman numerals, and various systems for filing papers, or catalogues, and various library systems, of which the Dewey Decimal _____ is an example. This still fits with the definition of components which are connected together (in this case in order to facilitate the flow of information.)

Chapter 1. Vectors

a. System
b. BIBO stability
c. 15 theorem
d. BDDC

32. In mathematics, the _____ of a function y = f(x) is a function that, in some fashion, 'undoes' the effect of f The _____ of f is denoted f^{-1}. The statements y=f(x) and x=f^{-1}(y) are equivalent.
    a. Inverse
    b. ACTRAN
    c. AUSM
    d. ALGOR

33. Let S be a set with a binary operation * . If e is an identity element of (S, *) and a * b = e, then a is called a _____ of b and b is called a right inverse of a. If an element x is both a _____ and a right inverse of y, then x is called a two-sided inverse, or simply an inverse, of y.
    a. Completing the square
    b. Hurwitz quaternion order
    c. Closed-form expression
    d. Left inverse

34. A _____ is one of the most curvilinear basic geometric shapes:It has two faces, zero vertices, and zero edges. The surface formed by the points at a fixed distance from a given straight line, the axis of the _____. The solid enclosed by this surface and by two planes perpendicular to the axis is also called a _____.
    a. Cylinder
    b. 15 theorem
    c. BDDC
    d. Right circular cylinder

35. If a particular point on a sphere is (arbitrarily) designated as its _____, then the corresponding antipodal point is called the south pole and the equator is the great circle that is equidistant to them. Great circles through the two poles are called lines (or meridians) of longitude, and the line connecting the two poles is called the axis of rotation. Circles on the sphere that are parallel to the equator are lines of latitude.
    a. North pole
    b. Tangent line
    c. Minimal surface
    d. Sphere

36. In geometry, an _____ is a plane curve produced by tracing the path of a chosen point of a circle -- called epicycle -- which rolls without slipping around a fixed circle. It is a particular kind of roulette.

If the smaller circle has radius r, and the larger circle has radius R = kr, then the parametric equations for the curve can be given by either:

$$x(\theta) = (R+r)\cos\theta - r\cos\left(\frac{R+r}{r}\theta\right)$$
$$y(\theta) = (R+r)\sin\theta - r\sin\left(\frac{R+r}{r}\theta\right),$$

or:

$$x(\theta) = r(k+1)\cos\theta - r\cos((k+1)\theta)$$
$$y(\theta) = r(k+1)\sin\theta - r\sin((k+1)\theta).$$

If k is an integer, then the curve is closed, and has k cusps (i.e., sharp corners, where the curve is not differentiable.)

a. ALGOR
b. Asymptotic curve
c. Epicycloid
d. ACTRAN

37. In geometry, a _____ is a special plane curve generated by the trace of a fixed point on a small circle that rolls within a larger circle. It is comparable to the cycloid but instead of the circle rolling along a line, it rolls within a circle. The red curve is a _____ traced as the smaller black circle rolls around inside the larger blue circle (parameters are R=3.0, r=1.0, and so k=3), giving a deltoid.

If the smaller circle has radius r, and the larger circle has radius R = kr, then the parametric equations for the curve can be given by either:

$$x(\theta) = (R-r)\cos\theta + r\cos\left(\frac{R-r}{r}\theta\right)$$
$$y(\theta) = (R-r)\sin\theta - r\sin\left(\frac{R-r}{r}\theta\right),$$

or:

$$x(\theta) = r(k-1)\cos\theta + r\cos((k-1)\theta)$$
$$y(\theta) = r(k-1)\sin\theta - r\sin((k-1)\theta).$$

If k is an integer, then the curve is closed, and has k cusps (i.e., sharp corners, where the curve is not differentiable.)

a. Kappa curve
b. Bullet-nose curve
c. Hypocycloid
d. Closed curve

1. In mathematics, the _____ (or replacement set) of a given function is the set of 'input' values for which the function is defined. For instance, the _____ of cosine would be all real numbers, while the _____ of the square root would be only numbers greater than or equal to 0 (ignoring complex numbers in both cases.) In a representation of a function in a xy Cartesian coordinate system, the _____ is represented on the x axis (or abscissa.)
    a. 15 theorem
    b. BIBO stability
    c. BDDC
    d. Domain

2. In elementary mathematics, physics, and engineering, a _____ is a geometric object that has both a magnitude (or length), direction and sense, (i.e., orientation along the given direction.) A _____ is frequently represented by a line segment with a definite direction, or graphically as an arrow, connecting an initial point A with a terminal point B, and denoted by

   The magnitude of the _____ is the length of the segment and the direction characterizes the displacement of B relative to A: how much one should move the point A to 'carry' it to the point B.

   Many algebraic operations on real numbers have close analogues for vectors.

    a. 15 theorem
    b. Vector
    c. BDDC
    d. Linear partial differential operator

3. In mathematics, a function f is said to be surjective or _____, if its values span its whole codomain; that is, for every y in the codomain, there is at least one x in the domain such that $f(x) = y$.

   Said another way, a function $f: X \to Y$ is surjective if and only if its range $f(X)$ is equal to its codomain Y. A surjective function is called a surjection.

   - For any set X, the identity function id_X on X is surjective.
   - The function $f: R \to R$ defined by $f(x) = 2x + 1$ is surjective (and even bijective), because for every real number y we have an x such that $f(x) = y$: an appropriate x is $(y - 1)/2$.
   - The natural logarithm function $\ln: (0,+\infty) \to R$ is surjective.
   - The function $f: Z \to \{0,1,2,3\}$ defined by $f(x) = x \mod 4$ is surjective.
   - The function $g: R \to R$ defined by $g(x) = x^2$ is not surjective, because (for example) there is no real number x such that $x^2 = -1$. However, the function $g: R \to [0,+\infty)$ defined by $g(x) = x^2$ (with restricted codomain) is surjective.

Chapter 2. Differentiation in Several Variables

Every function with a right inverse is a surjection. The converse is equivalent to the axiom of choice.

a. Injective function
b. One-to-one
c. Onto
d. One-to-one function

4. In mathematics, the _____ of a function is the set of all 'output' values produced by that function. Sometimes it is called the image, or more precisely, the image of the domain of the function. If a function is a surjection then its _____ is equal to its codomain.

a. Piecewise-defined function
b. Constant function
c. Surjective
d. Range

5. In mathematics, a function f is said to be _____ or onto, if its values span its whole codomain; that is, for every y in the codomain, there is at least one x in the domain such that f(x) = y.

Said another way, a function f: X → Y is _____ if and only if its range f(X) is equal to its codomain Y. A _____ function is called a surjection.

- For any set X, the identity function id_X on X is _____.
- The function f: R → R defined by f(x) = 2x + 1 is _____, because for every real number y we have an x such that f(x) = y: an appropriate x is (y - 1)/2.
- The natural logarithm function ln: (0,+∞) → R is _____.
- The function f: Z → {0,1,2,3} defined by f(x) = x mod 4 is _____.
- The function g: R → R defined by $g(x) = x^2$ is not _____, because (for example) there is no real number x such that $x^2 = -1$. However, the function g: R → [0,+∞) defined by $g(x) = x^2$ (with restricted codomain) is _____.

Every function with a right inverse is a surjection. The converse is equivalent to the axiom of choice.

a. Range
b. Constant function
c. Piecewise-defined function
d. Surjective

Chapter 2. Differentiation in Several Variables

6. In economics, the _____ functional form of production functions is widely used to represent the relationship of an output to inputs. It was proposed by Knut Wicksell (1851-1926), and tested against statistical evidence by Charles Cobb and Paul Douglas in 1900-1928.

For production, the function is

$$Y = AL^\alpha K^\beta,$$

where:

- Y = total production (the monetary value of all goods produced in a year)
- L = labor input
- K = capital input
- A = total factor productivity
- α and β are the output elasticities of labor and capital, respectively. These values are constants determined by available technology.

Output elasticity measures the responsiveness of output to a change in levels of either labor or capital used in production, ceteris paribus. For example if α = 0.15, a 1% increase in labor would lead to approximately a 0.15% increase in output.

a. Cobb-Douglas
b. 15 theorem
c. BIBO stability
d. BDDC

7. A _____ is a special kind of space curve, i.e. a smooth curve in three-space. As a mental image of a _____ one may take the spring (although the spring is not a curve, and so is technically not a _____, it does give a convenient mental picture.) A _____ is characterised by the fact that the tangent line at any point makes a constant angle with a fixed line.
a. BIBO stability
b. Helix
c. 15 theorem
d. BDDC

8. In mathematics, a (topological) _____ is defined as follows: let I be an interval of real numbers (i.e. a non-empty connected subset of $\mathbb{R}$); then a _____ γ is a continuous mapping $\gamma : I \to X$, where X is a topological space. The _____ γ is said to be simple if it is injective, i.e. if for all x, y in I, we have $\gamma(x) = \gamma(y) \implies x = y$. If I is a closed bounded interval $[a, b]$, we also allow the possibility $\gamma(a) = \gamma(b)$ (this convention makes it possible to talk about closed simple _____.)

a. Tractrix
b. Prolate cycloid
c. Curve
d. Closed curve

9. When the number of variables is two, this is a _____, if it is three this is a level surface, and for higher values of n the level set is a level hypersurface.

More specifically, a _____ is the set of all real-valued roots of an equation in two variables x_1 and x_2. A level surface is the set of all real-valued roots of an equation in three variables x_1, x_2 and x_3.

a. Multipole moment
b. Level curve
c. Scalar field
d. Partial derivative

10. A _____ is a statement of the meaning of a word or phrase. The term to be defined is known as the definiendum. The words which define it are known as the definiens.
a. 15 theorem
b. Definition
c. BIBO stability
d. BDDC

11. The _____ is a doubly ruled surface shaped like a saddle. In a suitable coordinate system, it can be represented by the equation

$$z = \frac{x^2}{a^2} - \frac{y^2}{b^2}.$$

This is a _____ that opens up along the x-axis and down along the y-axis.

Paraboloid of revolution

With a = b an elliptic paraboloid is a paraboloid of revolution: a surface obtained by revolving a parabola around its axis.

a. Paraboloid
b. Hyperbolic paraboloid
c. Parametric surface
d. Torus

12. In mathematics, a _____ is a quadric surface of special kind. There are two kinds of paraboloids: elliptic and hyperbolic. The elliptic _____ is shaped like an oval cup and can have a maximum or minimum point.
    a. Paraboloid
    b. Torus
    c. PDE surfaces
    d. Hyperbolic paraboloid

13. A _____ is perfectly round geometrical object in three-dimensional space, such as the shape of a round ball. Like a circle in two dimensions, a perfect _____ is completely symmetrical around its center, with all points on the surface lying the same distance r from the center point. This distance r is known as the radius of the _____.
    a. North pole
    b. Minimal surface
    c. Tangent line
    d. Sphere

14. An _____ is a type of quadric surface that is a higher dimensional analogue of an ellipse. The equation of a standard axis-aligned _____ body in an xyz-Cartesian coordinate system is

$$\frac{x^2}{a^2} + \frac{y^2}{b^2} + \frac{z^2}{c^2} = 1$$

where a and b are the equatorial radii (along the x and y axes) and c is the polar radius (along the z-axis), all of which are fixed positive real numbers determining the shape of the _____.

More generally, a not-necessarily-axis-aligned _____ is defined by the equation

$$\mathbf{x}^T A \mathbf{x} = 1$$

where A is a symmetric positive definite matrix and x is a vector.

Chapter 2. Differentiation in Several Variables

a. AUSM
b. Ellipsoid
c. ALGOR
d. ACTRAN

15. In mathematics, a hyperboloid is a quadric, a type of surface in three dimensions, described by the equation

$$\frac{x^2}{a^2} + \frac{y^2}{b^2} - \frac{z^2}{c^2} = 1 \underline{\qquad},$$

or

$$-\frac{x^2}{a^2} - \frac{y^2}{b^2} + \frac{z^2}{c^2} = 1 \text{ hyperboloid of two sheets.}$$

These are also called elliptical hyperboloids. If, and only if, a = b, it is a hyperboloid of revolution, and is also called a circular hyperboloid.

a. BIBO stability
b. 15 theorem
c. Hyperboloid of one sheet
d. BDDC

16. The _____ is the equation of state of a hypothetical ideal gas, first stated by Benoît Paul Émile Clapeyron in 1834. The law is derived from the fact that in the ideal state of any gas a given number of its 'particles' occupy the same volume, and that volume changes are inverse to pressure changes and linear to temperature changes.

The state of an amount of gas is determined by its pressure, volume, and temperature according to the equation:

$$pV = nRT$$

where

p is the absolute pressure of the gas,
V is the volume of the gas,
n is the number of moles of gas,
R is the universal gas constant,
T is the absolute temperature.

Chapter 2. Differentiation in Several Variables

   a. Ideal gas law
   b. ACTRAN
   c. AUSM
   d. ALGOR

17. In mathematics, the concept of a '_____' is used to describe the behavior of a function as its argument or input either 'gets close' to some point, or as the argument becomes arbitrarily large; or the behavior of a sequence's elements as their index increases indefinitely. Limits are used in calculus and other branches of mathematical analysis to define derivatives and continuity.

In formulas, _____ is usually abbreviated as lim

   a. 15 theorem
   b. BIBO stability
   c. BDDC
   d. Limit

18. In metric topology and related fields of mathematics, a set U is called _____ if, intuitively speaking, starting from any point x in U one can move by a small amount in any direction and still be in the set U. In other words, the distance between any point x in U and the edge of U is always greater than zero.

As an example, consider the _____ interval (0, 1) consisting of all real numbers x with 0 < x < 1. Here, the topology is the usual topology on the real line. We can look at this in two ways.

   a. ACTRAN
   b. Open
   c. AUSM
   d. ALGOR

19. In calculus, a branch of mathematics, the _____ is a measurement of how a function changes when its input changes. Loosely speaking, a _____ can be thought of as how much a quantity is changing at some given point. For example, the _____ of the position (or distance) of a vehicle with respect to time is the instantaneous velocity (respectively, instantaneous speed) at which the vehicle is traveling.

The process of finding a _____ is called differentiation. The fundamental theorem of calculus states that differentiation is the reverse process to integration.

Chapter 2. Differentiation in Several Variables

a. Semi-differentiability
b. Bounded function
c. Derivative
d. Stationary phase approximation

20. In mathematics, a _____ of a function of several variables is its derivative with respect to one of those variables with the others held constant (as opposed to the total derivative, in which all variables are allowed to vary.) Partial derivatives are useful in vector calculus and differential geometry.

The _____ of a function f with respect to the variable x is written as f'_x, $\partial_x f$, or $\partial f/\partial x$.

a. Jacobian
b. Level curve
c. Differentiation operator
d. Partial derivative

21. In geometry, the _____ (or simply the tangent) to a curve at a given point is the straight line that 'just touches' the curve at that point (in the sense explained more precisely below.) As it passes through the point of tangency, the _____ is 'going in the same direction' as the curve, and in this sense it is the best straight-line approximation to the curve at that point. The same definition applies to space curves and curves in n-dimensional Euclidean space.

a. North pole
b. Minimal surface
c. Tangent line
d. Lie derivative

22. f'(x) is twice the absolute value function, and it does not have a derivative at zero. Similar examples show that a function can have k derivatives for any non-negative integer k but no (k + 1)-order derivative. A function that has k successive derivatives is called _____.

a. Power series
b. Differential calculus
c. K times differentiable
d. Differential coefficient

23. In vector calculus, the _____ of a scalar field is a vector field which points in the direction of the greatest rate of increase of the scalar field, and whose magnitude is the greatest rate of change.

A generalization of the _____ for functions on a Euclidean space which have values in another Euclidean space is the Jacobian. A further generalization for a function from one Banach space to another is the Fréchet derivative.

a. Gradient
b. Smooth function
c. Lin-Tsien equation
d. Symmetric derivative

24. A _____ officer is an officer of high military rank. The term or equivalent is used by nearly every country in the world. _____ can be used as a generic term for all grades of _____ officer, or it can specifically refer to a single rank that is just called _____.

a. BDDC
b. BIBO stability
c. 15 theorem
d. General

25. In calculus, the _____ is a formula used to find the derivatives of products of functions. It may be stated thus:

$$(f \cdot g)' = f' \cdot g + f \cdot g'$$

or in the Leibniz notation thus:

$$\frac{d}{dx}(u \cdot v) = u \cdot \frac{dv}{dx} + v \cdot \frac{du}{dx}.$$

Discovery of this rule is credited to Gottfried Leibniz, who demonstrated it using differentials. Here is Leibniz's argument: Let u and v be two differentiable functions of x.

a. Differentiation rules
b. Quotient Rule
c. Constant factor rule in differentiation
d. Product rule

26. In calculus, the _____ is a method of finding the derivative of a function that is the quotient of two other functions for which derivatives exist.

Chapter 2. Differentiation in Several Variables

If the function one wishes to differentiate, f(x), can be written as

$$f(x) = \frac{g(x)}{h(x)}$$

and h(x) ≠ 0, then the rule states that the derivative of g(x) / h(x) is equal to:

$$\frac{d}{dx}f(x) = f'(x) = \frac{g'(x)h(x) - g(x)h'(x)}{[h(x)]^2}.$$

Or, more precisely, if all x in some open set containing the number a satisfy h(x) ≠ 0; and g'(a) and h'(a) both exist; then, f'(a) exists as well and:

$$f'(a) = \frac{g'(a)h(a) - g(a)h'(a)}{[h(a)]^2}.$$

The derivative of (4x − 2) / (x² + 1) is:

$$\frac{d}{dx}\left[\frac{(4x-2)}{x^2+1}\right] = \frac{(x^2+1)(4) - (4x-2)(2x)}{(x^2+1)^2}$$

$$= \frac{(4x^2+4) - (8x^2-4x)}{(x^2+1)^2} \qquad = \frac{-4x^2+4x+4}{(x^2+1)^2}$$

In the example above, the choices

g(x) = 4x − 2
h(x) = x² + 1

were made. Analogously, the derivative of sin(x) / x² (when x ≠ 0) is:

$$\frac{\cos(x)x^2 - \sin(x)2x}{x^4}$$

Another example is:

$$f(x) = \frac{2x^2}{x^3}$$

whereas g(x) = 2x² and h(x) = x³, and g'(x) = 4x and h'(x) = 3x².

a. Differentiation rules
b. Reciprocal Rule
c. Constant factor rule in differentiation
d. Quotient rule

27. In mathematics a _____ is a construction in vector calculus which associates a vector to every point in a (locally) Euclidean space.

Vector fields are often used in physics to model, for example, the speed and direction of a moving fluid throughout space, or the strength and direction of some force, such as the magnetic or gravitational force, as it changes from point to point.

In the rigorous mathematical treatment, (tangent) vector fields are defined on manifolds as sections of a manifold's tangent bundle.

a. Vector field
b. 15 theorem
c. BIBO stability
d. BDDC

28. A _____ is a mathematical function that maps real numbers to vectors. Vector-valued functions can be defined as:

- $\mathbf{r}(t) = f(t)\hat{\mathbf{i}} + g(t)\hat{\mathbf{j}}$ or
- $\mathbf{r}(t) = f(t)\hat{\mathbf{i}} + g(t)\hat{\mathbf{j}} + h(t)\hat{\mathbf{k}}$

where f(t), g(t) and h(t) are the coordinate functions of the parameter t, and $\hat{\mathbf{i}}$, $\hat{\mathbf{j}}$, and $\hat{\mathbf{k}}$ are unit vectors. r(t) is a vector which has its tail at the origin and its head at the coordinates evaluated by the function.

The vector shown in the graph to the right is the evaluation of the function near t=19.5 (between 6π and 6.5π; i.e., somewhat more than 3 rotations.)

Chapter 2. Differentiation in Several Variables

a. Direction vector
b. Direction cosines
c. Scalar multiplication
d. Vector-valued function

29. Smooth functions with given closed support are used in the construction of smooth partitions of unity ; these are essential in the study of smooth manifolds, for example to show that Riemannian metrics can be defined globally starting from their local existence. A simple case is that of a bump function on the real line, that is, a _____ f that takes the value 0 outside an interval [a,b] and such that

f(x) > 0 for a < x < b.

Given a number of overlapping intervals on the line, bump functions can be constructed on each of them, and on semi-infinite intervals (->∞, c] and [d,+>∞) to cover the whole line, such that the sum of the functions is always 1.

a. Symmetric derivative
b. Continuously differentiable
c. Gradient
d. Smooth function

30. Let S be a set with a binary operation * . If e is an identity element of (S, *) and a * b = e, then a is called a _____ of b and b is called a right inverse of a. If an element x is both a _____ and a right inverse of y, then x is called a two-sided inverse, or simply an inverse, of y.
    a. Hurwitz quaternion order
    b. Closed-form expression
    c. Completing the square
    d. Left inverse

31. Integration is an important concept in mathematics, specifically in the field of calculus and, more broadly, mathematical analysis. Given a function f of a real variable x and an interval [a, b] of the real line, the _____

$$\int_a^b f(x)\, dx,$$

is defined informally to be the net signed area of the region in the xy-plane bounded by the graph of f, the x-axis, and the vertical lines x = a and x = b.

The term '_____' may also refer to the notion of antiderivative, a function F whose derivative is the given function f.

a. Integrand
b. Integral test for convergence
c. Integral
d. Indefinite integral

32. When a polynomial is expressed as a sum or difference of terms (e.g., in standard or canonical form), the exponent of the term with the highest exponent is the _____. The degree of a term is the sum of the powers of each variable in the term. The words degree and order are used interchangeably.
   a. Quadratic polynomial
   b. Symmetric function
   c. Binomial type
   d. Degree of the polynomial

33. In acoustics and telecommunication, a _____ of a wave is a component frequency of the signal that is an integer multiple of the fundamental frequency. For example, if the fundamental frequency is f, the harmonics have frequencies f, 2f, 3f, 4f, etc. The harmonics have the property that they are all periodic at the fundamental frequency, therefore the sum of harmonics is also periodic at that frequency.
   a. BDDC
   b. Harmonic
   c. BIBO stability
   d. 15 theorem

34. In mathematics, mathematical physics and the theory of stochastic processes, a _____ is a twice continuously differentiable function f : U → R (where U is an open subset of R^n) which satisfies Laplace's equation, i.e.

$$\frac{\partial^2 f}{\partial x_1^2} + \frac{\partial^2 f}{\partial x_2^2} + \cdots + \frac{\partial^2 f}{\partial x_n^2} = 0$$

everywhere on U. This is also often written as

$$\nabla^2 f = 0 \quad \text{or} \quad \Delta f = 0.$$

There also exists a seemingly weaker definition that is equivalent. Indeed a function is harmonic if and only if it is weakly harmonic.

Harmonic functions can be defined on an arbitrary Riemannian manifold, using the Laplace-de Rham operator Δ.

a. Harmonic function
b. Maximum principle
c. Kelvin transform
d. Pluriharmonic function

35. The _____ is an important partial differential equation which describes the distribution of heat (or variation in temperature) in a given region over time. For a function u(x,y,z,t) of three spatial variables (x,y,z) and the time variable t, the _____ is

$$\frac{\partial u}{\partial t} - k\left(\frac{\partial^2 u}{\partial x^2} + \frac{\partial^2 u}{\partial y^2} + \frac{\partial^2 u}{\partial z^2}\right) = 0$$

or equivalently

$$\frac{\partial u}{\partial t} = k\nabla^2 u$$

where k is a constant.

The _____ is of fundamental importance in diverse scientific fields.

a. 15 theorem
b. BDDC
c. BIBO stability
d. Heat equation

36. The _____, after the plane and the catenoid, is the third minimal surface to be known. It was first discovered by Jean Baptiste Meusnier in 1776. Its name derives from its similarity to the helix: for every point on the _____ there is a helix contained in the _____ which passes through that point.

a. 15 theorem
b. Scherk surface
c. BDDC
d. Helicoid

37. In mathematics, a _____ is a surface with a mean curvature of zero. These include, but are not limited to, surfaces of minimum area subject to various constraints.

Physical models of area-minimizing minimal surfaces can be made by dipping a wire frame into a soap solution, forming a soap film, which is a _____ whose boundary is the wire frame.

a. Tortuosity
b. Tangent line
c. Differentiable manifold
d. Minimal surface

38. In mathematics and mathematical physics, _____ may be defined as the study of harmonic functions.

The term '_____' arises from the fact that, in 19th-century physics, the fundamental forces of nature were believed to be derived from potentials which satisfied Laplace's equation. Hence, _____ was the study of functions which could serve as potentials.

a. Multipole expansion
b. Dirichlet problem
c. Quadrature domain
d. Potential theory

39. In a totally ordered set all elements are mutually comparable, so such a set can have at most one minimal element and at most one maximal element. Then, due to mutual comparability, the minimal element will also be the least element and the maximal element will also be the greatest element. Thus in a totally ordered set we can simply use the terms minimum and _____.

a. Maximum
b. Leibniz rule
c. Nth term
d. Racetrack principle

40. In calculus, the _____ is a formula for the derivative of the composite of two functions.

In intuitive terms, if a variable, y, depends on a second variable, u, which in turn depends on a third variable, x, then the rate of change of y with respect to x can be computed as the rate of change of y with respect to u multiplied by the rate of change of u with respect to x. Schematically,

$$\frac{dy}{dx} = \frac{dy}{du} \cdot \frac{du}{dx}.$$

Chapter 2. Differentiation in Several Variables 29

a. Differentiation rules
b. Reciprocal Rule
c. Chain rule
d. Product rule

41. In mathematics, a _____ (or critical number) is a point on the domain of a function where:

- one dimension: the derivative (or slope of the line when visualized) is equal to zero or a point where the function ceases to be differentiable.
- in general: there are two distinct concepts: either the derivative (Jacobian) vanishes, or it is not of full rank (or, in either case, the function is not differentiable); these agree in one dimension.

Note that in one dimension, a critical value or critical number x of function f is the domain element at which the derivative is zero or undefined, whereas the associated ordered pair (x, y) is the _____. In higher dimensions a critical value is in the range whereas a _____ is in the domain.

There are two situations in which a point becomes a _____ of a function of one variable. The first of which is that the value of the first derivative is equal to zero.

a. Multivariable calculus
b. Critical point
c. Total derivative
d. Differentiation operator

42. In infinitesimal calculus, a _____ is traditionally an infinitesimally small change in a variable. For example, if x is a variable, then a change in the value of x is often denoted Δx (or δx when this change is considered to be small.) The _____ dx represents such a change, but is infinitely small.

a. Local maximum
b. Differential
c. Dirichlet integral
d. The Method of Mechanical Theorems

43. In mathematics, a _____ is an operator defined as a function of the differentiation operator. It is helpful, as a matter of notation first, to consider differentiation as an abstract operation, accepting a function and returning another (in the style of a higher-order function in computer science.)

There are certainly reasons not to restrict to linear operators; for instance the Schwarzian derivative is a well-known non-linear operator.

a. Surface integral
b. Differential operator
c. Parametric equations
d. Critical point

44. In differential geometry there are a number of second-order, linear, elliptic differential operators bearing the name _____.

The connection _____ is a differential operator acting on the various tensor bundles of a manifold, defined in terms of a Riemmanian- or pseudo-Riemannian metric.

a. Semi-elliptic operator
b. Peetre theorem
c. Laplacian
d. Dirac operator

45. In mathematics, the _____ of a multivariate differentiable function along a given vector V at a given point P intuitively represents the instantaneous rate of change of the function, moving through P, in the direction of V. It therefore generalizes the notion of a partial derivative, in which the direction is always taken parallel to one of the coordinate axes.

The _____ is a special case of the Gâteaux derivative.

The _____ of a scalar function $f(\vec{x}) = f(x_1, x_2, \ldots, x_n)$ along a vector $\vec{v} = (v_1, \ldots, v_n)$ is the function defined by the limit

<_____> $$\nabla_{\vec{v}} f(\vec{x}) = \lim_{h \to 0} \frac{f(\vec{x} + h\vec{v}) - f(\vec{x})}{h}.$$

Sometimes authors write D_v instead of ∇_v.

a. Directional derivative
b. Linearity of differentiation
c. Symmetrically continuous
d. Differentiation of trigonometric functions

46. In mathematics, an _____ is a generalization for the concept of a function in which the dependent variable has not been given 'explicitly' in terms of the independent variable. To give a function f explicitly is to provide a prescription for determining the output value of the function y in terms of the input value x:

Chapter 2. Differentiation in Several Variables

y = f(x.)

By contrast, the function is implicit if the value of y is obtained from x by solving an equation of the form:

R(x,y) = 0.

a. Ordinary differential equation
b. Automatic differentiation
c. Implicit differentiation
d. Implicit function

47. In the branch of mathematics called multivariable calculus, the _____ is a tool which allows relations to be converted to functions. It does this by representing the relation as the graph of a function. There may not be a single function whose graph is the entire relation, but there may be such a function on a restriction of the domain of the relation.
    a. Implicit function theorem
    b. Inverse function theorem
    c. Upper convected time derivative
    d. Isoperimetric inequality

48. In vector calculus, the _____ is shorthand for either the _____ matrix or its determinant, the _____ determinant.

In algebraic geometry the _____ of a curve means the _____ variety: a group variety associated to the curve, in which the curve can be embedded.

These concepts are all named after the mathematician Carl Gustav Jacob Jacobi.

   a. Critical point
   b. Saddle surface
   c. Jacobian
   d. Vector Laplacian

49. In mathematics, the _____ of a function y = f(x) is a function that, in some fashion, 'undoes' the effect of f The _____ of f is denoted f^{-1}. The statements y=f(x) and x=f^{-1}(y) are equivalent.

a. ACTRAN
b. ALGOR
c. AUSM
d. Inverse

50. In mathematics, if f is a function from A to B then an _____ for f is a function in the opposite direction, from B to A, with the property that a round trip (a composition) from A to B to A (or from B to A to B) returns each element of the initial set to itself. Thus, if an input x into the function f produces an output y, then inputting y into the _____ f^{-1} (read f inverse, not to be confused with exponentiation) produces the output x. Not every function has an inverse; those that do are called invertible.

a. Inverse function
b. Augustin-Jean Fresnel
c. Augustin Louis Cauchy
d. Aristotle

51. In mathematics, specifically differential calculus, the _____ gives sufficient conditions for a function to be invertible in a neighborhood of a point in its domain. The theorem also gives a formula for the derivative of the inverse function.

In multivariable calculus, this theorem can be generalized to any vector-valued function whose Jacobian determinant is nonzero at a point in its domain.

a. Upper convected time derivative
b. Inverse function theorem
c. Isoperimetric inequality
d. Implicit function theorem

52. In the two-dimensional case, a _____ perpendicularly intersects the tangent line to a curve at a given point.

The _____ is often used in computer graphics to determine a surface's orientation toward a light source for flat shading, or the orientation of each of the corners (vertices) to mimic a curved surface with Phong shading.

For a polygon (such as a triangle), a surface normal can be calculated as the vector cross product of two (non-parallel) edges of the polygon.

a. Hyperbolic paraboloid
b. PDE surfaces
c. Parametric surface
d. Normal line

Chapter 2. Differentiation in Several Variables

53. In mathematics, a _____ is a curve in a Euclidian plane (cf. space curve.) The most frequently studied cases are smooth plane curves (including piecewise smooth plane curves), and algebraic plane curves.
    a. Lipschitz domain
    b. Plane curve
    c. Vector area
    d. Gyroid

54. In the mathematical field of numerical analysis, a _____ is a parametric curve important in computer graphics and related fields. Generalizations of Bezier curves to higher dimensions are called Bezier surfaces, of which the Bezier triangle is a special case.

    Bezier curves were widely publicized in 1962 by the French engineer Pierre B>ézier, who used them to design automobile bodies.

    a. BIBO stability
    b. 15 theorem
    c. BDDC
    d. Bezier curve

55. The _____ is an important second-order linear partial differential equation that describes the propagation of a variety of waves, such as sound waves, light waves and water waves. It arises in fields such as acoustics, electromagnetics, and fluid dynamics. Historically, the problem of a vibrating string such as that of a musical instrument was studied by Jean le Rond d'Alembert, Leonhard Euler, Daniel Bernoulli, and Joseph-Louis Lagrange.
    a. Volume
    b. Wave equation
    c. Lagrangian
    d. Dirac equation

56. In mathematics, a _____ is a function with multiplicative scaling behaviour: if the argument is multiplied by a factor, then the result is multiplied by some power of this factor.

    Suppose that $f : V \to W$ is a function between two vector spaces over a field F.

    We say that f is homogeneous of degree k if

    $$f(\alpha \mathbf{v}) = \alpha^k f(\mathbf{v})$$

    for all nonzero $\alpha \in F$ and $\mathbf{v} \in V$.

Chapter 2. Differentiation in Several Variables

a. Direction vector
b. Homogeneous function
c. Direction cosines
d. Dot product

57. In physics, and more specifically kinematics, _____ is the change in velocity over time. Because velocity is a vector, it can change in two ways: a change in magnitude and/or a change in direction. In one dimension, _____ is the rate at which something speeds up or slows down.
    a. Acceleration
    b. AUSM
    c. ACTRAN
    d. ALGOR

58. In mathematics, the hyperbolic functions are analogs of the ordinary trigonometric functions. The basic hyperbolic functions are the hyperbolic sine 'sinh', and the _____ 'cosh', from which are derived the hyperbolic tangent 'tanh', etc., in analogy to the derived trigonometric functions. The inverse hyperbolic functions are the area hyperbolic sine 'arsinh' (also called 'asinh', or sometimes by the misnomer of 'arcsinh') and so on.
    a. Hyperbolic tangent
    b. Step function
    c. Hyperbolic cosine
    d. Square root function

59. In physics, _____ is defined as the rate of change of position. it is vector physical quantity; both speed and direction are required to define it. In the SI (metric) system, it is measured in meters per second: (m/s) or ms^{-1}.
    a. 15 theorem
    b. BDDC
    c. Velocity
    d. BIBO stability

60. _____ was a German mathematician, astronomer and astrologer, and key figure in the 17th century scientific revolution. He is best known for his eponymous laws of planetary motion, codified by later astronomers based on his works Astronomia nova, Harmonices Mundi, and Epitome of Copernican Astrononomy. They also provided one of the foundations for Isaac Newton's theory of universal gravitation.

Chapter 2. Differentiation in Several Variables

a. Niels Henrik David Bohr
b. Johannes Kepler
c. MÄ dhava of Sangamagrama
d. Robin K. Bullough

61. In geometry, a _____ (pl. tori) is a surface of revolution generated by revolving a circle in three dimensional space about an axis coplanar with the circle, which does not touch the circle. Examples of tori include the surfaces of doughnuts and inner tubes.
    a. Hyperbolic paraboloid
    b. Torus
    c. Prolate
    d. Paraboloid

62. _____ is the long dimension of any object. The _____ of a thing is the distance between its ends, its linear extent as measured from end to end. This may be distinguished from height, which is vertical extent, and width or breadth, which are the distance from side to side, measuring across the object at right angles to the _____.
    a. Length
    b. BDDC
    c. 15 theorem
    d. BIBO stability

63. In calculus, an _____, primitive or indefinite integral of a function f is a function F whose derivative is equal to f, i.e., F >' = f. The process of solving for antiderivatives is antidifferentiation (or indefinite integration.) Antiderivatives are related to definite integrals through the fundamental theorem of calculus: the definite integral of a function over an interval is equal to the difference between the values of an _____ evaluated at the endpoints of the interval.
    a. Indefinite integral
    b. Order of integration
    c. Integrand
    d. Antiderivative

64. In mathematics, _____ refers to any of a number of loosely related concepts in different areas of geometry. Intuitively, _____ is the amount by which a geometric object deviates from being flat, or straight in the case of a line, but this is defined in different ways depending on the context. There is a key distinction between extrinsic _____, which is defined for objects embedded in another space (usually a Euclidean space) in a way that relates to the radius of _____ of circles that touch the object, and intrinsic _____, which is defined at each point in a differential manifold.

a. Minimal surface
b. Curvature
c. Sphere
d. Lie derivative

65. A surface normal to a flat surface is a vector which is perpendicular to that surface. A normal to a non-flat surface at a point P on the surface is a vector perpendicular to the tangent plane to that surface at P. The word 'normal' is also used as an adjective: a line normal to a plane, the normal component of a force, the _____, etc. The concept of normality generalizes to orthogonality.

a. Normal line
b. Normal vector
c. Paraboloid
d. Hyperbolic paraboloid

66. In mathematics, an _____ is a particular type of curve: a hypocycloid with four cusps. Astroids are also superellipses: all astroids are scaled versions of the curve specified by the equation

$$x^{2/3} + y^{2/3} = 1.$$

Its modern name comes from the Greek word for 'star'.

a. ACTRAN
b. Astroid
c. ALGOR
d. Epicycloid

67. In mathematics, a _____ is a method for approximating the total area underneath a curve on a graph, otherwise known as an integral. It may also be used to define the integration operation.

Consider a function $f: D \rightarrow \mathbf{R}$, where D is a subset of the real numbers $\mathbf{R}$, and let $I = [a, b]$ be a closed interval contained in D. A finite set of points $\{x_0, x_1, x_2, \ldots x_n\}$ such that $a = x_0 < x_1 < x_2 \ldots < x_n = b$ creates a partition

$P = \{[x_0, x_1], [x_1, x_2], \ldots [x_{n-1}, x_n]\}$

of I.

a. Solid of revolution
b. Risch algorithm
c. Signed measure
d. Riemann sum

68. In mathematics and physics, a _____ associates a scalar value, which can be either mathematical in definition to every point in space. Scalar fields are often used in physics, for instance to indicate the temperature distribution throughout space or more specifically, differential geometry, the set of functions defined on a manifold define the commutative ring of functions.
    a. Symmetry of second derivatives
    b. Level curve
    c. Vector Laplacian
    d. Scalar field

69. _____ or isopotential in mathematics and physics (especially electronics) refers to a region in space where every point in it is at the same potential. This usually refers to a scalar potential, although it can also be applied to vector potentials. Often, _____ surfaces are used to visualize an (n)-dimensional scalar potential function in (n-1) dimensional space.
    a. Upper convected time derivative
    b. Implicit function theorem
    c. Inverse function theorem
    d. Equipotential

70. _____ are surfaces of constant scalar potential. They are used to visualize an (n)-dimensional scalar potential function in (n-1) dimensional space. The gradient of the potential, denoting the direction of greatest increase, is perpendicular to the surface.
    a. ALGOR
    b. ACTRAN
    c. Integration by reduction formulae
    d. Equipotential surfaces

71. A vector field V defined on a set S is called a _____ or a conservative field if there exists a real valued function (a scalar field) f on S such that

$$V = \nabla f.$$

The associated flow is called the gradient flow, and is used in the method of gradient descent.

The path integral along any closed curve γ (γ(0) = γ(1)) in a _____ is zero:

$$\int_\gamma \langle V(x), dx \rangle = \int_\gamma \langle \nabla f(x), dx \rangle = f(\gamma(1)) - f(\gamma(0))$$

a. BDDC
b. 15 theorem
c. BIBO stability
d. Gradient field

72. In vector calculus, _____ is a vector differential operator represented by the nabla symbol: ∇.

_____ is a mathematical tool serving primarily as a convention for mathematical notation; it makes many equations easier to comprehend, write, and remember. Depending on the way _____ is applied, it can describe the gradient (slope), divergence (degree to which something converges or diverges) or curl (rotational motion at points in a fluid.)

a. Green's theorem
b. Divergence Theorem
c. Triple product
d. Del

73. In vector calculus, the _____ is an operator that measures the magnitude of a vector field's source or sink at a given point; the _____ of a vector field is a (signed) scalar. For example, consider air as it is heated or cooled. The relevant vector field for this example is the velocity of the moving air at a point.

a. Gradient theorem
b. Triple product
c. Green's theorem
d. Divergence

74. In applied mathematics and the calculus of variations, the _____ of a functional $J(y)$ is defined as $\delta J(y) = \dfrac{d}{d\varepsilon} J(y + \varepsilon h) \big|_{\varepsilon=0}$, where y and h are functions.

Compute the _____ of $$J(y) = \int_a^b yy' dx$$

a. Maupertuis' principle
b. Lagrange multipliers on Banach spaces
c. First variation
d. Hu-Washizu principle

75. In vector calculus a _____ vector field (also known as an incompressible vector field) is a vector field v with divergence zero:

$$\nabla \cdot \mathbf{v} = 0.$$

The fundamental theorem of vector calculus states that any vector field can be expressed as the sum of a conservative vector field and a _____ field. The condition of zero divergence is satisfied whenever a vector field v has only a vector potential component, because the definition of the vector potential A as:

$$\mathbf{v} = \nabla \times \mathbf{A}$$

automatically results in the identity (as can be shown, for example, using Cartesian coordinates):

$$\nabla \cdot \mathbf{v} = \nabla \cdot (\nabla \times \mathbf{A}) = 0.$$

The converse also holds: for any _____ v there exists a vector potential A such that $\mathbf{V} = \nabla \times \mathbf{A}$.

The divergence theorem, gives the equivalent integral definition of a _____ field; namely that for any closed surface S, the net total flux through the surface must be zero:

$$\iint_S \mathbf{v} \cdot d\mathbf{s} = 0$$

where $d\mathbf{s}$ is the outward normal to each surface element.

a. Principal part
b. Bloch space
c. Trigonometric series
d. Solenoidal

Chapter 2. Differentiation in Several Variables

76. In vector calculus a conservative vector field is a vector field which is the gradient of a scalar potential. There are two closely related concepts: path independence and _____ vector fields. Every conservative vector field has zero curl (and is thus _____), and every conservative vector field has the path independence property.
   a. AUSM
   b. ALGOR
   c. Irrotational
   d. ACTRAN

77. In mathematics and its applications, a _____ system is a system for assigning an n-tuple of numbers or scalars to each point in an n-dimensional space. This concept is part of the theory of manifolds. 'Scalars' in many cases means real numbers, but, depending on context, can mean complex numbers or elements of some other commutative ring.
   a. 15 theorem
   b. Cylindrical coordinate system
   c. Spherical coordinate system
   d. Coordinate

78. A _____ is one of the most curvilinear basic geometric shapes:It has two faces, zero vertices, and zero edges. The surface formed by the points at a fixed distance from a given straight line, the axis of the _____. The solid enclosed by this surface and by two planes perpendicular to the axis is also called a _____.
   a. Cylinder
   b. BDDC
   c. 15 theorem
   d. Right circular cylinder

79. If a particular point on a sphere is (arbitrarily) designated as its _____, then the corresponding antipodal point is called the south pole and the equator is the great circle that is equidistant to them. Great circles through the two poles are called lines (or meridians) of longitude, and the line connecting the two poles is called the axis of rotation. Circles on the sphere that are parallel to the equator are lines of latitude.
   a. Tangent line
   b. Sphere
   c. North pole
   d. Minimal surface

80. _____ is the curve along which a small object moves, under the influence of friction, when pulled on a horizontal plane by a piece of thread and a puller that moves at a right angle to the initial line between the object and the puller at an infinitesimal speed. It is therefore a curve of pursuit. It was first introduced by Claude Perrault in 1670, and later studied by Sir Isaac Newton and Christian Huygens (1692.)

a. Folium of Descartes
b. Curve
c. Bullet-nose curve
d. Tractrix

81. _____, S(x) and C(x), are two transcendental functions named after Augustin-Jean Fresnel that are used in optics. They arise in the description of near field Fresnel diffraction phenomena, and are defined through the following integral representations:

$$S(x) = \int_0^x \sin(t^2)\, dt, \quad C(x) = \int_0^x \cos(t^2)\, dt.$$

The simultaneous parametric plot of S(x) and C(x) is the Cornu spiral, or clothoid.

Normalised _____, S(x) and C(x).
 a. First derivative test
 b. Differential
 c. Leibniz function
 d. Fresnel integrals

82. Typically the pair u and v are taken to be the real and imaginary parts of a complex-valued function f(x + iy) = u(x,y) + iv (x,y.) Suppose that u and v are continuously differentiable on an open subset of C. Then f = u+iv is holomorphic if and only if the partial derivatives of u and v satisfy the _____ and (1b.)

The equations are one way of looking at the condition on a function to be differentiable (holomorphic) in the sense of complex analysis: in other words they encapsulate the notion of function of a complex variable by means of conventional differential calculus.

a. Spherical harmonics
b. Solid harmonics
c. Viscosity solution
d. Cauchy-Riemann equations

83. _____ is a PDE solver of Maxwell's equations based on the method of moments. It is a 3-D planar electromagnetic (EM) simulator used for passive circuit analysis. It is presently marketed by Agilent Technologies EEsof division , but the tool was original developed by a Belgian company, Alphabit, a spinoff from IMEC, which was acquired by Hewlett-Packard and later spun out as part of Agilent.

Chapter 2. Differentiation in Several Variables

   a. Geometric integrator
   b. Finite-difference time-domain
   c. Forward-Time Central-Space
   d. Momentum

84. _____ is the tendency of a force to rotate an object about an axis (or fulcrum or pivot.) Just as a force is a push or a pull, a _____ can be thought of as a twist. The symbol for _____ is τ, the Greek letter tau.
   a. BDDC
   b. 15 theorem
   c. BIBO stability
   d. Torque

85. In calculus, _____ gives a sequence of approximations of a differentiable function around a given point by polynomials (the Taylor polynomials of that function) whose coefficients depend only on the derivatives of the function at that point. The theorem also gives precise estimates on the size of the error in the approximation. The theorem is named after the mathematician Brook Taylor, who stated it in 1712, though the result was first discovered 41 years earlier in 1671 by James Gregory.
   a. Related rates
   b. Taylor's theorem
   c. Fresnel integrals
   d. Local minimum

86. In a totally ordered set all elements are mutually comparable, so such a set can have at most one minimal element and at most one maximal element. Then, due to mutual comparability, the minimal element will also be the least element and the maximal element will also be the greatest element. Thus in a totally ordered set we can simply use the terms _____ and maximum.
   a. Nth term
   b. Ghosts of departed quantities
   c. Minimum
   d. Maximum

87. In mathematics, a _____ is a point in the domain of a function of two variables which is a stationary point but not a local extremum. At such a point, in general, the surface resembles a saddle that curves up in one direction, and curves down in a different direction (like a mountain pass.) In terms of contour lines, a _____ can be recognized, in general, by a contour that appears to intersect itself.

a. BIBO stability
b. BDDC
c. Saddle point
d. 15 theorem

88. Let f be a differentiable function, and let f'(x) be its derivative. The derivative of f'(x) (if it has one) is written f''(x) and is called the _____ of f. Similarly, the derivative of a _____, if it exists, is written f'''(x) and is called the third derivative of f.

a. Stationary phase approximation
b. Vertical asymptote
c. Second derivative
d. Slant asymptote

89. In calculus, a branch of mathematics, the _____ is a criterion often useful for determining whether a given stationary point of a function is a local maximum or a local minimum.

The test states: If the function f is twice differentiable at a stationary point x, meaning that $f'(x) = 0$, then:

- If $f''(x) < 0$ then f has a local maximum at x.
- If $f''(x) > 0$ then f has a local minimum at x.
- If $f''(x) = 0$, the _____ says nothing about the point x, has a possible inflection point.

In the last case, the function may have a local maximum or minimum there, but the function is sufficiently 'flat' that this is undetected by the second derivative. In this case one has to examine the third derivative. Such an example is f(x) = x⁴.

a. Second derivative test
b. Stationary point
c. Symmetric derivative
d. Linearity of differentiation

90. In mathematics, a _____ is an ordered list of objects (or events). Like a set, it contains members (also called elements or terms), and the number of terms (possibly infinite) is called the length of the _____. Unlike a set, order matters, and the exact same elements can appear multiple times at different positions in the _____.

a. 15 theorem
b. Sequence
c. Slope
d. Y-intercept

91. The largest and the smallest element of a set are called extreme values, absolute extrema, or extreme records.

For a differentiable function f, if f(x_0) is an _____ for the set of all values f(x), and if x_0 is in the interior of the domain of f, then x_0 is a critical point, by Fermat's theorem.

In the case of a general partial order one should not confuse a least element (smaller than all other) and a minimal element (nothing is smaller.)

a. Integration by substitution
b. Extreme value
c. Extreme Value Theorem
d. Infinitesimal

92. In calculus, the _____ states that if a real-valued function f is continuous in the closed and bounded interval [a,b], then f must attain its maximum and minimum value, each at least once. That is, there exist numbers c and d in [a,b] such that:

$$f(c) \geq f(x) \geq f(d) \quad \text{for all } x \in [a, b].$$

A related theorem is the boundedness theorem which states that a continuous function f in the closed interval [a,b] is bounded on that interval. That is, there exist real numbers m and M such that:

$$m \leq f(x) \leq M \quad \text{for all } x \in [a, b].$$

The _____ enriches the boundedness theorem by saying that not only is the function bounded, but it also attains its least upper bound as its maximum and its greatest lower bound as its minimum.

a. Uniform convergence
b. Infinitesimal
c. Integral of secant cubed
d. Extreme value theorem

Chapter 2. Differentiation in Several Variables

93. In mathematical optimization, the method of Lagrange multipliers provides a strategy for finding the maximum/minimum of a function subject to constraints.

For example, consider the optimization problem

$$\text{maximize } f(x, y)$$
$$\text{subject to } g(x, y) = c.$$

We introduce a new variable (λ) called a _____, and study the Lagrange function defined by

$$\Lambda(x, y, \lambda) = f(x, y) - \lambda\big(g(x, y) - c\big).$$

If (x,y)′ is a maximum for the original constrained problem, then there exists a λ such that (x,y,λ)′ is a stationary point for the Lagrange function (stationary points are those points where the partial derivatives of Λ are zero.) However, not all stationary points yield a solution of the original problem.

a. Lagrange multiplier
b. BIBO stability
c. BDDC
d. 15 theorem

94. The method of _____ or ordinary _____ is used to solve overdetermined systems. _____ is often applied in statistical contexts, particularly regression analysis.

_____ can be interpreted as a method of fitting data. The best fit in the _____ sense is that instance of the model for which the sum of squared residuals has its least value, a residual being the difference between an observed value and the value given by the model.

a. BDDC
b. BIBO stability
c. 15 theorem
d. Least squares

95. In statistics, _____ is a form of regression analysis in which the relationship between one or more independent variables and another variable, called dependent variable, is modeled by a least squares function, called _____ equation. This function is a linear combination of one or more model parameters, called regression coefficients. A _____ equation with one independent variable represents a straight line.

a. Probability
b. Correlation
c. Linear regression
d. Standard deviation

96. In vector calculus a _____ is a vector field which is the gradient of a scalar potential. There are two closely related concepts: path independence and irrotational vector fields. Every _____ has zero curl (and is thus irrotational), and every _____ has the path independence property.

a. Divergence Theorem
b. Del
c. Green's theorem
d. Conservative vector field

97. In mathematics, the point $\tilde{x} \in \mathbb{R}^n$ is an _____ for the differential equation

$$\frac{d\mathbf{x}}{dt} = \mathbf{f}(t, \mathbf{x})$$

if $\mathbf{f}(t, \tilde{\mathbf{x}}) = 0$ for all t.

Similarly, the point $\tilde{x} \in \mathbb{R}^n$ is an _____ (or fixed point) for the difference equation

$$\mathbf{x}_{k+1} = \mathbf{f}(k, \mathbf{x}_k)$$

if $\mathbf{f}(k, \tilde{\mathbf{x}}) = \tilde{\mathbf{x}}$ for $k = 0, 1, 2, \ldots$.

Equilibria can be classified by looking at the signs of the eigenvalues of the linearization of the equations about the equilibria.

a. AUSM
b. ACTRAN
c. ALGOR
d. Equilibrium point

98. The _____ of an object is the extra energy which it possesses due to its motion. It is defined as the work needed to accelerate a body of a given mass from rest to its current velocity. Having gained this energy during its acceleration, the body maintains this _____ unless its speed changes.

Chapter 2. Differentiation in Several Variables

a. Kinetic energy
b. 15 theorem
c. Law of Conservation of Energy
d. BDDC

99. _____ can be thought of as energy stored within a physical system. It is called _____ because it has the potential to be converted into other forms of energy, such as kinetic energy, and to do work in the process. The standard (SI) unit of measure for _____ is the joule, the same as for work or energy in general.

a. BDDC
b. Potential energy
c. Law of Conservation of Energy
d. 15 theorem

100. In vector calculus, a _____ is a vector field whose curl is a given vector field. This is analogous to a scalar potential, which is a scalar field whose negative gradient is a given vector field.

Formally, given a vector field v, a _____ is a vector field A such that

$$\mathbf{v} = \nabla \times \mathbf{A}.$$

If a vector field v admits a _____ A, then from the equality

$$\nabla \cdot (\nabla \times \mathbf{A}) = 0$$

(divergence of the curl is zero) one obtains

$$\nabla \cdot \mathbf{v} = \nabla \cdot (\nabla \times \mathbf{A}) = 0,$$

which implies that v must be a solenoidal vector field.

a. Vector potential
b. Lagrangian
c. Moment of Inertia
d. Wave equation

101. In mathematics and statistics, the _____ of a list of numbers is the sum of all of the list divided by the number of items in the list. If the list is a statistical population, then the mean of that population is called a population mean. If the list is a statistical sample, we call the resulting statistic a sample mean.

a. ACTRAN
b. ALGOR
c. AUSM
d. Arithmetic mean

102. In probability theory and statistics, the _____ (or expectation value or mean and for continuous random variables with a density function it is the probability density -weighted integral of the possible values.

The term '_____' can be misleading.

a. ALGOR
b. ACTRAN
c. AUSM
d. Expected value

103. The _____, in mathematics, is a type of mean or average, which indicates the central tendency or typical value of a set of numbers. It is similar to the arithmetic mean, which is what most people think of with the word 'average,' except that instead of adding the set of numbers and then dividing the sum by the count of numbers in the set, n, the numbers are multiplied and then the nth root of the resulting product is taken.

For instance, the _____ of two numbers, say 2 and 8, is just the square root (i.e., the second root) of their product, 16, which is 4.

a. Geometric mean
b. Continuous random variable
c. Normal distribution
d. Standard deviation

Chapter 3. Multiple Integration

1. The _____ of any solid, liquid, plasma, vacuum or theoretical object is how much three-dimensional space it occupies, often quantified numerically. One-dimensional figures (such as lines) and two-dimensional shapes (such as squares) are assigned zero _____ in the three-dimensional space. _____ is commonly presented in units such as mL or cm³ (milliliters or cubic centimeters.)
   a. Dirac equation
   b. Klein-Gordon equation
   c. Vector potential
   d. Volume

2. Integration is an important concept in mathematics, specifically in the field of calculus and, more broadly, mathematical analysis. Given a function f of a real variable x and an interval [a, b] of the real line, the _____

$$\int_a^b f(x)\, dx,$$

is defined informally to be the net signed area of the region in the xy-plane bounded by the graph of f, the x-axis, and the vertical lines x = a and x = b.

The term '_____' may also refer to the notion of antiderivative, a function F whose derivative is the given function f.

   a. Indefinite integral
   b. Integral test for convergence
   c. Integrand
   d. Integral

3. In mathematics, a _____ is a method for approximating the total area underneath a curve on a graph, otherwise known as an integral. It may also be used to define the integration operation.

Consider a function $f: D \longrightarrow \mathbf{R}$, where D is a subset of the real numbers $\mathbf{R}$, and let $I = [a, b]$ be a closed interval contained in D. A finite set of points $\{x_0, x_1, x_2, \ldots x_n\}$ such that $a = x_0 < x_1 < x_2 \ldots < x_n = b$ creates a partition

$$P = \{[x_0, x_1), [x_1, x_2), \ldots [x_{n-1}, x_n]\}$$

of I.

a. Risch algorithm
b. Riemann sum
c. Solid of revolution
d. Signed measure

4. Just as the definite integral of a positive function of one variable represents the area of the region between the graph of the function and the x-axis, the _____ of a positive function of two variables represents the volume of the region between the surface defined by the function (on the three dimensional Cartesian plane where z = f(x,y)) and the plane which contains its domain. (Note that the same volume can be obtained via the triple integral -- the integral of a function in three variables -- of the constant function f(x, y, z) = 1 over the above-mentioned region between the surface and the plane.) If there are more variables, a multiple integral will yield hypervolumes of multi-dimensional functions.
    a. Constant of integration
    b. Risch algorithm
    c. Trigonometric substitution
    d. Double integral

5. In elementary mathematics, physics, and engineering, a _____ is a geometric object that has both a magnitude (or length), direction and sense, (i.e., orientation along the given direction.) A _____ is frequently represented by a line segment with a definite direction, or graphically as an arrow, connecting an initial point A with a terminal point B, and denoted by

The magnitude of the _____ is the length of the segment and the direction characterizes the displacement of B relative to A: how much one should move the point A to 'carry' it to the point B.

Many algebraic operations on real numbers have close analogues for vectors.

    a. Linear partial differential operator
    b. BDDC
    c. 15 theorem
    d. Vector

6. In economics, the _____ functional form of production functions is widely used to represent the relationship of an output to inputs. It was proposed by Knut Wicksell (1851-1926), and tested against statistical evidence by Charles Cobb and Paul Douglas in 1900-1928.

Chapter 3. Multiple Integration

For production, the function is

$$Y = AL^{\alpha}K^{\beta},$$

where:

- Y = total production (the monetary value of all goods produced in a year)
- L = labor input
- K = capital input
- A = total factor productivity
- α and β are the output elasticities of labor and capital, respectively. These values are constants determined by available technology.

Output elasticity measures the responsiveness of output to a change in levels of either labor or capital used in production, ceteris paribus. For example if α = 0.15, a 1% increase in labor would lead to approximately a 0.15% increase in output.

a. BIBO stability
b. Cobb-Douglas
c. 15 theorem
d. BDDC

7. In mathematics, a _____ is a function whose definition is dependent on the value of the independent variable. Mathematically, a real-valued function f of a real variable x is a relationship whose definition is given differently on disjoint subsets of its domain

The word piecewise is also used to describe any property of a _____ that holds for each piece but may not hold for the whole domain of the function.

a. Surjective
b. Piecewise-defined function
c. Constant function
d. Range

8. A _____ is a statement of the meaning of a word or phrase. The term to be defined is known as the definiendum . The words which define it are known as the definiens .

Chapter 3. Multiple Integration

    a. BDDC
    b. Definition
    c. 15 theorem
    d. BIBO stability

9. In probability theory and statistics, the _____ (or expectation value or mean and for continuous random variables with a density function it is the probability density -weighted integral of the possible values.

The term '_____' can be misleading.

    a. ALGOR
    b. AUSM
    c. ACTRAN
    d. Expected value

10. In calculus, the _____ states, roughly, that given a section of a smooth curve, there is at least one point on that section at which the derivative (slope) of the curve is equal (parallel) to the 'average' derivative of the section. It is used to prove theorems that make global conclusions about a function on an interval starting from local hypotheses about derivatives at points of the interval.

This theorem can be understood concretely by applying it to motion: If a car travels one hundred miles in one hour, so its average speed during that time was 100 miles per hour.

    a. Hyperbolic angle
    b. Periodic function
    c. Mean value theorem
    d. Limits of integration

11. In mathematics and its applications, a _____ system is a system for assigning an n-tuple of numbers or scalars to each point in an n-dimensional space. This concept is part of the theory of manifolds. 'Scalars' in many cases means real numbers, but, depending on context, can mean complex numbers or elements of some other commutative ring.
    a. Cylindrical coordinate system
    b. Coordinate
    c. Spherical coordinate system
    d. 15 theorem

12. In vector calculus, the _____ is shorthand for either the _____ matrix or its determinant, the _____ determinant.

Chapter 3. Multiple Integration

In algebraic geometry the _____ of a curve means the _____ variety: a group variety associated to the curve, in which the curve can be embedded.

These concepts are all named after the mathematician Carl Gustav Jacob Jacobi.

a. Saddle surface
b. Jacobian
c. Vector Laplacian
d. Critical point

13. In mathematics, a _____ is a basic technique used to simplify problems in which the original variables are replaced with new ones; the new and old variables being related in some specified way. The intent is that the problem expressed in new variables may be simpler, or else equivalent to a better understood problem.

A very simple example of a useful variable change can be seen in the problem of finding the roots of the eighth order polynomial:

$$x^8 + 3x^4 + 2 = 0$$

Eighth order polynomial equations are generally impossible to solve in terms of elementary functions.

a. Quadratic formula
b. Linear equation
c. Change of variables
d. Cubic function

14. In mathematics, the _____ is a two-dimensional coordinate system in which each point on a plane is determined by an angle and a distance. The _____ is especially useful in situations where the relationship between two points is most easily expressed in terms of angles and distance; in the more familiar Cartesian or rectangular coordinate system, such a relationship can only be found through trigonometric formulation.

As the coordinate system is two-dimensional, each point is determined by two polar coordinates: the radial coordinate and the angular coordinate.

a. 15 theorem
b. BIBO stability
c. Polar coordinate system
d. BDDC

15. A _____ officer is an officer of high military rank. The term or equivalent is used by nearly every country in the world. _____ can be used as a generic term for all grades of _____ officer, or it can specifically refer to a single rank that is just called _____.
   a. BIBO stability
   b. BDDC
   c. 15 theorem
   d. General

16. A _____ is one of the most curvilinear basic geometric shapes:It has two faces, zero vertices, and zero edges. The surface formed by the points at a fixed distance from a given straight line, the axis of the _____. The solid enclosed by this surface and by two planes perpendicular to the axis is also called a _____.
   a. 15 theorem
   b. Right circular cylinder
   c. BDDC
   d. Cylinder

17. If a particular point on a sphere is (arbitrarily) designated as its _____, then the corresponding antipodal point is called the south pole and the equator is the great circle that is equidistant to them. Great circles through the two poles are called lines (or meridians) of longitude, and the line connecting the two poles is called the axis of rotation. Circles on the sphere that are parallel to the equator are lines of latitude.
   a. Tangent line
   b. Minimal surface
   c. Sphere
   d. North pole

18. In mathematics, a _____ provides a means for integrating a function with respect to volume in various coordinate systems such as spherical coordinates and cylindrical coordinates. More generally, a _____ is a measure on a manifold.

On an orientable n-manifold, the _____ typically arises from a volume form: a differential form of degree n which is nowhere equal to zero.

   a. 15 theorem
   b. Volume element
   c. BIBO stability
   d. BDDC

Chapter 3. Multiple Integration

19. The concept of _____ in mathematics evolved from the concept of _____ in physics. The nth _____ of a real-valued function f(x) of a real variable about a value c is

$$\mu'_n = \int_{-\infty}^{\infty} (x-c)^n f(x)\, dx.$$

It is possible to define moments for random variables in a more general fashion than moments for real values. See Moments in metric spaces.

a. Geometric mean
b. Median
c. Poisson distribution
d. Moment

20. The _____ of a system of particles is a specific point at which, for many purposes, the system's mass behaves as if it were concentrated. The _____ is a function only of the positions and masses of the particles that comprise the system. In the case of a rigid body, the position of its _____ is fixed in relation to the object (but not necessarily in contact with it.)

a. Simple harmonic motion
b. Center of mass
c. Fundamental lemma in the calculus of variations
d. 15 theorem

21. In mathematical optimization, the method of Lagrange multipliers provides a strategy for finding the maximum/minimum of a function subject to constraints.

For example, consider the optimization problem

$$\text{maximize } f(x, y)$$
$$\text{subject to } g(x, y) = c.$$

We introduce a new variable (λ) called a _____, and study the Lagrange function defined by

$$\Lambda(x, y, \lambda) = f(x, y) - \lambda\big(g(x, y) - c\big).$$

If (x,y)′ is a maximum for the original constrained problem, then there exists a λ such that (x,y,λ)′ is a stationary point for the Lagrange function (stationary points are those points where the partial derivatives of Λ are zero.) However, not all stationary points yield a solution of the original problem.

a. BIBO stability
b. BDDC
c. Lagrange multiplier
d. 15 theorem

22. In geometry, the _____, geometric center, or barycenter of a plane figure X is the intersection of all straight lines that divide X into two parts of equal moment about the line. Informally, it is the 'average' of all points of X. The definition extends to any object X in n-dimensional space: its _____ is the intersection of all hyperplanes that divide X into two parts of equal moment.
   a. BDDC
   b. 15 theorem
   c. BIBO stability
   d. Centroid

23. _____ is the name of several related measures of the size of an object, a surface, or an ensemble of points. It is calculated as the root mean square distance of the objects' parts from either its center of gravity or an axis.

In structural engineering, the two-dimensional _____ is used to describe the distribution of cross sectional area in a beam around its centroidal axis.

   a. BDDC
   b. Radius of gyration
   c. 15 theorem
   d. BIBO stability

24. _____ is the tendency of a force to rotate an object about an axis (or fulcrum or pivot.) Just as a force is a push or a pull, a _____ can be thought of as a twist. The symbol for _____ is τ, the Greek letter tau.
   a. BIBO stability
   b. 15 theorem
   c. Torque
   d. BDDC

25. In calculus, an _____ is the limit of a definite integral as an endpoint of the interval of integration approaches either a specified real number or ∞ or −∞ or, in some cases, as both endpoints approach limits.

Chapter 3. Multiple Integration

Specifically, an _____ is a limit of the form

$$\lim_{b \to \infty} \int_a^b f(x)\, dx, \qquad \lim_{a \to -\infty} \int_a^b f(x)\, dx,$$

or of the form

$$\lim_{c \to b^-} \int_a^c f(x)\, dx, \qquad \lim_{c \to a^+} \int_c^b f(x)\, dx,$$

in which one takes a limit in one or the other (or sometimes both) endpoints. Improper integrals may also occur at an interior point of the domain of integration, or at multiple such points.

a. ACTRAN
b. AUSM
c. Improper integral
d. ALGOR

26. The _____ of a material is defined as its mass per unit volume. The symbol of _____ is ρ ('>rho.)

Mathematically:

$$d = \frac{m}{V}$$

where:

    d is the _____,
    m is the mass,
    V is the volume.

a. BIBO stability
b. Density
c. 15 theorem
d. BDDC

27. A _____ is the location at which two or more bones make contact. They are constructed to allow movement and provide mechanical support, and are classified structurally and functionally. Depiction of an intervertebral disk, a cartilaginous _____. Diagram of a synovial (diarthrosis) _____.

Joints are mainly classified structurally and functionally.

a. BDDC
b. 15 theorem
c. BIBO stability
d. Joint

28. _____ is a way of expressing knowledge or belief that an event will occur or has occurred. In mathematics the concept has been given an exact meaning in _____ theory, that is used extensively in such areas of study as mathematics, statistics, finance, gambling, science, and philosophy to draw conclusions about the likelihood of potential events and the underlying mechanics of complex systems.

The word _____ does not have a consistent direct definition.

a. Probability
b. Normal distribution
c. Discrete probability distributions
d. Linear regression

29. In mathematics a _____ is a construction in vector calculus which associates a vector to every point in a (locally) Euclidean space.

Vector fields are often used in physics to model, for example, the speed and direction of a moving fluid throughout space, or the strength and direction of some force, such as the magnetic or gravitational force, as it changes from point to point.

In the rigorous mathematical treatment, (tangent) vector fields are defined on manifolds as sections of a manifold's tangent bundle.

a. 15 theorem
b. BDDC
c. BIBO stability
d. Vector field

Chapter 4. Line Integrals

1. In mathematics, a _____ is an integral where the function to be integrated is evaluated along a curve. Various different line integrals are in use. A specific case of an integration along a closed curve in two dimensions or the complex plane is the contour integral.
    a. Picard theorem
    b. Line integral
    c. Mittag-Leffler star
    d. Radius of convergence

2. Integration is an important concept in mathematics, specifically in the field of calculus and, more broadly, mathematical analysis. Given a function f of a real variable x and an interval [a, b] of the real line, the _____

$$\int_a^b f(x)\, dx,$$

is defined informally to be the net signed area of the region in the xy-plane bounded by the graph of f, the x-axis, and the vertical lines x = a and x = b.

The term '_____' may also refer to the notion of antiderivative, a function F whose derivative is the given function f.

   a. Indefinite integral
   b. Integrand
   c. Integral
   d. Integral test for convergence

3. In elementary mathematics, physics, and engineering, a _____ is a geometric object that has both a magnitude (or length), direction and sense, (i.e., orientation along the given direction.) A _____ is frequently represented by a line segment with a definite direction, or graphically as an arrow, connecting an initial point A with a terminal point B, and denoted by

The magnitude of the _____ is the length of the segment and the direction characterizes the displacement of B relative to A: how much one should move the point A to 'carry' it to the point B.

Many algebraic operations on real numbers have close analogues for vectors.

a. 15 theorem
b. Linear partial differential operator
c. BDDC
d. Vector

4. In geometry, the _____ (or simply the tangent) to a curve at a given point is the straight line that 'just touches' the curve at that point (in the sense explained more precisely below.) As it passes through the point of tangency, the _____ is 'going in the same direction' as the curve, and in this sense it is the best straight-line approximation to the curve at that point. The same definition applies to space curves and curves in n-dimensional Euclidean space.

a. North pole
b. Minimal surface
c. Lie derivative
d. Tangent line

5. In infinitesimal calculus, a _____ is traditionally an infinitesimally small change in a variable. For example, if x is a variable, then a change in the value of x is often denoted Δx (or δx when this change is considered to be small.) The _____ dx represents such a change, but is infinitely small.

a. Local maximum
b. The Method of Mechanical Theorems
c. Dirichlet integral
d. Differential

6. In the mathematical fields of differential geometry and tensor calculus, differential forms are an approach to multivariable calculus that is independent of coordinates. A _____ of degree k, or (differential) k-form, on a smooth manifold M is a smooth section of the kth exterior power of the cotangent bundle of M. The set of all k-forms on M is a vector space commonly denoted $\Omega^k(M).$

A differential 0-form is by definition a smooth function on M. A differential 1-form is an object dual to a vector field on M.

a. Two-form
b. Hodge dual
c. Soldering
d. Differential form

Chapter 4. Line Integrals

7. In mathematics, a (topological) _____ is defined as follows: let I be an interval of real numbers (i.e. a non-empty connected subset of $\mathbb{R}$); then a _____ γ is a continuous mapping $\gamma : I \to X$, where X is a topological space. The _____ γ is said to be simple if it is injective, i.e. if for all x, y in I, we have $\gamma(x) = \gamma(y) \implies x = y$. If I is a closed bounded interval $[a, b]$, we also allow the possibility $\gamma(a) = \gamma(b)$ (this convention makes it possible to talk about closed simple _____.)
   a. Closed curve
   b. Prolate cycloid
   c. Tractrix
   d. Curve

8. In mathematics, an _____ on a real vector space is a choice of which ordered bases are 'positively' oriented and which are 'negatively' oriented. In the three-dimensional Euclidean space, the two possible basis orientations are called right-handed and left-handed (or right-chiral and left-chiral), respectively. However, the choice of _____ is independent of the handedness or chirality of the bases (although right-handed bases are typically declared to be positively oriented, they may also be assigned a negative _____.)
   a. ACTRAN
   b. Unit vector
   c. ALGOR
   d. Orientation

9. For an orientable surface, a consistent choice of 'clockwise' (as opposed to counter-clockwise) is called an orientation, and the surface is called _____. An orientable surface admits exactly 2 orientations, and the distinction between an _____ surface and an orientable surface is subtle and frequently blurred. An orientable surface is an abstract surface that admits an orientation, while an _____ surface is a surface that is abstractly orientable, and has the additional datum of a choice of one of the 2 possible orientations.
   a. AUSM
   b. ALGOR
   c. ACTRAN
   d. Oriented

Chapter 4. Line Integrals

10. In the various subfields of physics, there exist two common usages of the term _____, both with rigorous mathematical frameworks.

   - In the study of transport phenomena (heat transfer, mass transfer and fluid dynamics), _____ is defined as the amount that flows through a unit area per unit time. _____ in this definition is a vector.
   - In the field of electromagnetism and mathematics, _____ is usually the integral of a vector quantity over a finite surface. The result of this integration is a scalar quantity. The magnetic _____ is thus the integral of the magnetic vector field B over a surface, and the electric _____ is defined similarly. Using this definition, the _____ of the Poynting vector over a specified surface is the rate at which electromagnetic energy flows through that surface. Confusingly, the Poynting vector is sometimes called the power _____, which is an example of the first usage of _____, above. It has units of watts per square metre (WÂ·m^{-2})

One could argue, based on the work of James Clerk Maxwell, that the transport definition precedes the more recent way the term is used in electromagnetism. The specific quote from Maxwell is 'In the case of fluxes, we have to take the integral, over a surface, of the _____ through every element of the surface. The result of this operation is called the surface integral of the _____.

   a. 15 theorem
   b. BIBO stability
   c. BDDC
   d. Flux

11. In economics, the _____ functional form of production functions is widely used to represent the relationship of an output to inputs. It was proposed by Knut Wicksell (1851-1926), and tested against statistical evidence by Charles Cobb and Paul Douglas in 1900-1928.

For production, the function is

$$Y = AL^{\alpha}K^{\beta},$$

where:

   - Y = total production (the monetary value of all goods produced in a year)
   - L = labor input
   - K = capital input
   - A = total factor productivity
   - α and β are the output elasticities of labor and capital, respectively. These values are constants determined by available technology.

Output elasticity measures the responsiveness of output to a change in levels of either labor or capital used in production, ceteris paribus. For example if α = 0.15, a 1% increase in labor would lead to approximately a 0.15% increase in output.

a. Cobb-Douglas
b. BIBO stability
c. 15 theorem
d. BDDC

12. In vector calculus a _____ is a vector field which is the gradient of a scalar potential. There are two closely related concepts: path independence and irrotational vector fields. Every _____ has zero curl (and is thus irrotational), and every _____ has the path independence property.

   a. Divergence Theorem
   b. Del
   c. Conservative vector field
   d. Green's theorem

13. In vector calculus, the _____ of a scalar field is a vector field which points in the direction of the greatest rate of increase of the scalar field, and whose magnitude is the greatest rate of change.

A generalization of the _____ for functions on a Euclidean space which have values in another Euclidean space is the Jacobian. A further generalization for a function from one Banach space to another is the Fréchet derivative.

   a. Symmetric derivative
   b. Smooth function
   c. Lin-Tsien equation
   d. Gradient

14. In mathematics a _____ is a construction in vector calculus which associates a vector to every point in a (locally) Euclidean space.

Vector fields are often used in physics to model, for example, the speed and direction of a moving fluid throughout space, or the strength and direction of some force, such as the magnetic or gravitational force, as it changes from point to point.

In the rigorous mathematical treatment, (tangent) vector fields are defined on manifolds as sections of a manifold's tangent bundle.

Chapter 4. Line Integrals

a. BDDC
b. 15 theorem
c. Vector field
d. BIBO stability

15. In mathematics, a _____ is a method for approximating the total area underneath a curve on a graph, otherwise known as an integral. It may also be used to define the integration operation.

Consider a function $f: D \rightarrow R$, where D is a subset of the real numbers R, and let $I = [a, b]$ be a closed interval contained in D. A finite set of points $\{x_0, x_1, x_2, ... x_n\}$ such that $a = x_0 < x_1 < x_2 ... < x_n = b$ creates a partition

$$P = \{[x_0, x_1), [x_1, x_2), ... [x_{n-1}, x_n]\}$$

of I.

a. Riemann sum
b. Risch algorithm
c. Signed measure
d. Solid of revolution

16. _____ is the name of several related measures of the size of an object, a surface, or an ensemble of points. It is calculated as the root mean square distance of the objects' parts from either its center of gravity or an axis.

In structural engineering, the two-dimensional _____ is used to describe the distribution of cross sectional area in a beam around its centroidal axis.

a. BIBO stability
b. Radius of gyration
c. 15 theorem
d. BDDC

17. In calculus, a branch of mathematics, the _____ is a measurement of how a function changes when its input changes. Loosely speaking, a _____ can be thought of as how much a quantity is changing at some given point. For example, the _____ of the position (or distance) of a vehicle with respect to time is the instantaneous velocity (respectively, instantaneous speed) at which the vehicle is traveling.

The process of finding a _____ is called differentiation. The fundamental theorem of calculus states that differentiation is the reverse process to integration.

a. Derivative
b. Bounded function
c. Semi-differentiability
d. Stationary phase approximation

18. In acoustics and telecommunication, a _____ of a wave is a component frequency of the signal that is an integer multiple of the fundamental frequency. For example, if the fundamental frequency is f, the harmonics have frequencies f, 2f, 3f, 4f, etc. The harmonics have the property that they are all periodic at the fundamental frequency, therefore the sum of harmonics is also periodic at that frequency.

a. 15 theorem
b. BIBO stability
c. BDDC
d. Harmonic

19. In mathematics, mathematical physics and the theory of stochastic processes, a _____ is a twice continuously differentiable function f : U → R (where U is an open subset of R^n) which satisfies Laplace's equation, i.e.

$$\frac{\partial^2 f}{\partial x_1^2} + \frac{\partial^2 f}{\partial x_2^2} + \cdots + \frac{\partial^2 f}{\partial x_n^2} = 0$$

everywhere on U. This is also often written as

$$\nabla^2 f = 0 \quad \text{or} \quad \Delta f = 0.$$

There also exists a seemingly weaker definition that is equivalent. Indeed a function is harmonic if and only if it is weakly harmonic.

Harmonic functions can be defined on an arbitrary Riemannian manifold, using the Laplace-de Rham operator Δ.

a. Maximum principle
b. Kelvin transform
c. Harmonic function
d. Pluriharmonic function

20. In differential geometry there are a number of second-order, linear, elliptic differential operators bearing the name _____

The connection _____ is a differential operator acting on the various tensor bundles of a manifold, defined in terms of a Riemmanian- or pseudo-Riemannian metric.

a. Dirac operator
b. Peetre theorem
c. Semi-elliptic operator
d. Laplacian

21. The _____ states that the total amount of energy in an isolated system remains constant. A consequence of this law is that energy cannot be created or destroyed. The only thing that can happen with energy in an isolated system is that it can change form, that is to say for instance kinetic energy can become thermal energy.

a. Potential energy
b. BDDC
c. Law of conservation of energy
d. 15 theorem

Chapter 5. Surface Integrals and Vector Analysis

1. A _____ is a statement of the meaning of a word or phrase. The term to be defined is known as the definiendum. The words which define it are known as the definiens.
    a. BDDC
    b. BIBO stability
    c. 15 theorem
    d. Definition

2. In mathematics, a _____ is a method for approximating the total area underneath a curve on a graph, otherwise known as an integral. It may also be used to define the integration operation.

    Consider a function $f: D \rightarrow R$, where D is a subset of the real numbers R, and let $I = [a, b]$ be a closed interval contained in D. A finite set of points $\{x_0, x_1, x_2, ... x_n\}$ such that $a = x_0 < x_1 < x_2 ... < x_n = b$ creates a partition

    $P = \{[x_0, x_1), [x_1, x_2), ... [x_{n-1}, x_n]\}$

    of I.

    a. Solid of revolution
    b. Riemann sum
    c. Risch algorithm
    d. Signed measure

3. In mathematics, a (topological) _____ is defined as follows: let I be an interval of real numbers (i.e. a non-empty connected subset of $\mathbb{R}$); then a _____ γ is a continuous mapping $\gamma : I \to X$, where X is a topological space. The _____ γ is said to be simple if it is injective, i.e. if for all x, y in I, we have $\gamma(x) = \gamma(y) \implies x = y$. If I is a closed bounded interval $[a, b]$, we also allow the possibility $\gamma(a) = \gamma(b)$ (this convention makes it possible to talk about closed simple _____.)
    a. Prolate cycloid
    b. Tractrix
    c. Closed curve
    d. Curve

4. In geometry, a _____ (pl. tori) is a surface of revolution generated by revolving a circle in three dimensional space about an axis coplanar with the circle, which does not touch the circle. Examples of tori include the surfaces of doughnuts and inner tubes.

Chapter 5. Surface Integrals and Vector Analysis

a. Paraboloid
b. Hyperbolic paraboloid
c. Prolate
d. Torus

5. A surface normal to a flat surface is a vector which is perpendicular to that surface. A normal to a non-flat surface at a point P on the surface is a vector perpendicular to the tangent plane to that surface at P. The word 'normal' is also used as an adjective: a line normal to a plane, the normal component of a force, the _____, etc. The concept of normality generalizes to orthogonality.

a. Normal line
b. Hyperbolic paraboloid
c. Paraboloid
d. Normal vector

6. In elementary mathematics, physics, and engineering, a _____ is a geometric object that has both a magnitude (or length), direction and sense, (i.e., orientation along the given direction.) A _____ is frequently represented by a line segment with a definite direction, or graphically as an arrow, connecting an initial point A with a terminal point B, and denoted by

The magnitude of the _____ is the length of the segment and the direction characterizes the displacement of B relative to A: how much one should move the point A to 'carry' it to the point B.

Many algebraic operations on real numbers have close analogues for vectors.

a. Linear partial differential operator
b. 15 theorem
c. BDDC
d. Vector

7. In mathematics, a _____ is a function whose definition is dependent on the value of the independent variable. Mathematically, a real-valued function f of a real variable x is a relationship whose definition is given differently on disjoint subsets of its domain

The word piecewise is also used to describe any property of a _____ that holds for each piece but may not hold for the whole domain of the function.

a. Piecewise-defined function
b. Range
c. Surjective
d. Constant function

8. _____ is how much exposed area an object has. It is expressed in square units. If an object has flat faces, its _____ can be calculated by adding together the areas of its faces.
a. Plane curve
b. Lipschitz domain
c. Vector area
d. Surface area

9. The _____, after the plane and the catenoid, is the third minimal surface to be known. It was first discovered by Jean Baptiste Meusnier in 1776. Its name derives from its similarity to the helix: for every point on the _____ there is a helix contained in the _____ which passes through that point.
a. Scherk surface
b. 15 theorem
c. BDDC
d. Helicoid

10. Integration is an important concept in mathematics, specifically in the field of calculus and, more broadly, mathematical analysis. Given a function f of a real variable x and an interval [a, b] of the real line, the _____

$$\int_a^b f(x)\,dx,$$

is defined informally to be the net signed area of the region in the xy-plane bounded by the graph of f, the x-axis, and the vertical lines x = a and x = b.

The term '_____' may also refer to the notion of antiderivative, a function F whose derivative is the given function f.

a. Integral test for convergence
b. Integral
c. Integrand
d. Indefinite integral

Chapter 5. Surface Integrals and Vector Analysis

11. In mathematics, _____ are a method of defining a curve. A simple kinematical example is when one uses a time parameter to determine the position, velocity, and other information about a body in motion.

Abstractly, a relation is given in the form of an equation, and it is shown also to be the image of functions from items such as R^n.

   a. Shift theorem
   b. Partial derivative
   c. Critical point
   d. Parametric equations

12. In mathematics, a _____ is a definite integral taken over a surface (which may be a curved set in space); it can be thought of as the double integral analog of the line integral. Given a surface, one may integrate over it scalar fields (that is, functions which return numbers as values), and vector fields (that is, functions which return vectors as values.)

Surface integrals have applications in physics, particularly with the classical theory of electromagnetism.

   a. Surface integral
   b. Symmetry of second derivatives
   c. Differential operator
   d. Contact

13. In the various subfields of physics, there exist two common usages of the term _____, both with rigorous mathematical frameworks.

   - In the study of transport phenomena (heat transfer, mass transfer and fluid dynamics), _____ is defined as the amount that flows through a unit area per unit time. _____ in this definition is a vector.
   - In the field of electromagnetism and mathematics, _____ is usually the integral of a vector quantity over a finite surface. The result of this integration is a scalar quantity. The magnetic _____ is thus the integral of the magnetic vector field B over a surface, and the electric _____ is defined similarly. Using this definition, the _____ of the Poynting vector over a specified surface is the rate at which electromagnetic energy flows through that surface. Confusingly, the Poynting vector is sometimes called the power _____, which is an example of the first usage of _____, above. It has units of watts per square metre (WÂ·m^{-2})

One could argue, based on the work of James Clerk Maxwell, that the transport definition precedes the more recent way the term is used in electromagnetism. The specific quote from Maxwell is 'In the case of fluxes, we have to take the integral, over a surface, of the _____ through every element of the surface. The result of this operation is called the surface integral of the _____.

Chapter 5. Surface Integrals and Vector Analysis

a. BDDC
b. Flux
c. BIBO stability
d. 15 theorem

14. A surface S in the Euclidean space R³ is _____ if a two-dimensional figure (for example,) cannot be moved around the surface and back to where it started so that it looks like its own mirror image (.) Otherwise the surface is non-_____.

More precisely, and applicable to non-embedded surfaces, a surface is non-_____ if there is a continuous map f from the product of a 2-dimensional disk D and the unit interval [0,1] to the surface, $f : D \times [0, 1] \to S$ such that f(c,t) = f(d,t) only if c = d for every t in [0,1], and there exists a reflection map r such that f(d,0) = f(r(d),1) for every d in D.

a. AUSM
b. ALGOR
c. Orientable
d. ACTRAN

15. In mathematics, an _____ on a real vector space is a choice of which ordered bases are 'positively' oriented and which are 'negatively' oriented. In the three-dimensional Euclidean space, the two possible basis orientations are called right-handed and left-handed (or right-chiral and left-chiral), respectively. However, the choice of _____ is independent of the handedness or chirality of the bases (although right-handed bases are typically declared to be positively oriented, they may also be assigned a negative _____.)

a. ACTRAN
b. ALGOR
c. Unit vector
d. Orientation

16. For an orientable surface, a consistent choice of 'clockwise' (as opposed to counter-clockwise) is called an orientation, and the surface is called _____. An orientable surface admits exactly 2 orientations, and the distinction between an _____ surface and an orientable surface is subtle and frequently blurred. An orientable surface is an abstract surface that admits an orientation, while an _____ surface is a surface that is abstractly orientable, and has the additional datum of a choice of one of the 2 possible orientations.

a. ALGOR
b. Oriented
c. AUSM
d. ACTRAN

Chapter 5. Surface Integrals and Vector Analysis

17. The _____ of a material is defined as its mass per unit volume. The symbol of _____ is ρ '>rho.)

Mathematically:

$$d = \frac{m}{V}$$

where:

    d is the _____,
    m is the mass,
    V is the volume.

a. BDDC
b. BIBO stability
c. Density
d. 15 theorem

18. In vector calculus, the _____ is an operator that measures the magnitude of a vector field's source or sink at a given point; the _____ of a vector field is a (signed) scalar. For example, consider air as it is heated or cooled. The relevant vector field for this example is the velocity of the moving air at a point.
a. Green's theorem
b. Gradient theorem
c. Triple product
d. Divergence

19. In vector calculus, the _____ Ostrogradskye;s theorem the _____ states that the outward flux of a vector field through a surface is equal to the triple integral of the divergence on the region inside the surface. Intuitively, it states that the sum of all sources minus the sum of all sinks gives the net flow out of a region.
a. Green's theorem
b. Divergence theorem
c. Divergence
d. Del

20. In mathematics and its applications, a _____ system is a system for assigning an n-tuple of numbers or scalars to each point in an n-dimensional space. This concept is part of the theory of manifolds. 'Scalars' in many cases means real numbers, but, depending on context, can mean complex numbers or elements of some other commutative ring.

Chapter 5. Surface Integrals and Vector Analysis

73

a. 15 theorem
b. Spherical coordinate system
c. Cylindrical coordinate system
d. Coordinate

21. A _____ is one of the most curvilinear basic geometric shapes:It has two faces, zero vertices, and zero edges. The surface formed by the points at a fixed distance from a given straight line, the axis of the _____. The solid enclosed by this surface and by two planes perpendicular to the axis is also called a _____.
   a. Cylinder
   b. 15 theorem
   c. BDDC
   d. Right circular cylinder

22. In calculus, a branch of mathematics, the _____ is a measurement of how a function changes when its input changes. Loosely speaking, a _____ can be thought of as how much a quantity is changing at some given point. For example, the _____ of the position (or distance) of a vehicle with respect to time is the instantaneous velocity (respectively, instantaneous speed) at which the vehicle is traveling.

The process of finding a _____ is called differentiation. The fundamental theorem of calculus states that differentiation is the reverse process to integration.

   a. Stationary phase approximation
   b. Bounded function
   c. Semi-differentiability
   d. Derivative

23. If a particular point on a sphere is (arbitrarily) designated as its _____, then the corresponding antipodal point is called the south pole and the equator is the great circle that is equidistant to them. Great circles through the two poles are called lines (or meridians) of longitude, and the line connecting the two poles is called the axis of rotation. Circles on the sphere that are parallel to the equator are lines of latitude.
   a. Minimal surface
   b. Sphere
   c. Tangent line
   d. North pole

24. In differential geometry there are a number of second-order, linear, elliptic differential operators bearing the name _____.

Chapter 5. Surface Integrals and Vector Analysis

The connection _____ is a differential operator acting on the various tensor bundles of a manifold, defined in terms of a Riemmanian- or pseudo-Riemannian metric.

a. Laplacian
b. Dirac operator
c. Peetre theorem
d. Semi-elliptic operator

25. In acoustics and telecommunication, a _____ of a wave is a component frequency of the signal that is an integer multiple of the fundamental frequency. For example, if the fundamental frequency is f, the harmonics have frequencies f, 2f, 3f, 4f, etc. The harmonics have the property that they are all periodic at the fundamental frequency, therefore the sum of harmonics is also periodic at that frequency.

a. 15 theorem
b. BDDC
c. BIBO stability
d. Harmonic

26. In mathematics, mathematical physics and the theory of stochastic processes, a _____ is a twice continuously differentiable function f : U → R (where U is an open subset of R^n) which satisfies Laplace's equation, i.e.

$$\frac{\partial^2 f}{\partial x_1^2} + \frac{\partial^2 f}{\partial x_2^2} + \cdots + \frac{\partial^2 f}{\partial x_n^2} = 0$$

everywhere on U. This is also often written as

$$\nabla^2 f = 0 \quad \text{or} \quad \Delta f = 0.$$

There also exists a seemingly weaker definition that is equivalent. Indeed a function is harmonic if and only if it is weakly harmonic.

Harmonic functions can be defined on an arbitrary Riemannian manifold, using the Laplace-de Rham operator Δ.

a. Kelvin transform
b. Harmonic function
c. Maximum principle
d. Pluriharmonic function

Chapter 5. Surface Integrals and Vector Analysis

27. In infinitesimal calculus, a _____ is traditionally an infinitesimally small change in a variable. For example, if x is a variable, then a change in the value of x is often denoted Δx (or δx when this change is considered to be small.) The _____ dx represents such a change, but is infinitely small.

   a. The Method of Mechanical Theorems
   b. Local maximum
   c. Dirichlet integral
   d. Differential

28. In the mathematical fields of differential geometry and tensor calculus, differential forms are an approach to multivariable calculus that is independent of coordinates. A _____ of degree k, or (differential) k-form, on a smooth manifold M is a smooth section of the kth exterior power of the cotangent bundle of M. The set of all k-forms on M is a vector space commonly denoted $\Omega^k(M)$.

A differential 0-form is by definition a smooth function on M. A differential 1-form is an object dual to a vector field on M.

   a. Hodge dual
   b. Two-form
   c. Soldering
   d. Differential form

29. In economics, the _____ functional form of production functions is widely used to represent the relationship of an output to inputs. It was proposed by Knut Wicksell (1851-1926), and tested against statistical evidence by Charles Cobb and Paul Douglas in 1900-1928.

For production, the function is

   $Y = AL^\alpha K^\beta$,

where:

   - Y = total production (the monetary value of all goods produced in a year)
   - L = labor input
   - K = capital input
   - A = total factor productivity
   - α and β are the output elasticities of labor and capital, respectively. These values are constants determined by available technology.

Output elasticity measures the responsiveness of output to a change in levels of either labor or capital used in production, ceteris paribus. For example if α = 0.15, a 1% increase in labor would lead to approximately a 0.15% increase in output.

a. BIBO stability
b. Cobb-Douglas
c. 15 theorem
d. BDDC

30. A _____ is a differential equation that describes the conservative transport of some kind of quantity. Since mass, energy, momentum, and other natural quantities are conserved, a vast variety of physics may be described with continuity equations.

All the examples of continuity equations below express the same idea.

a. BDDC
b. BIBO stability
c. 15 theorem
d. Continuity equation

31. In vector calculus, a _____ is a vector field whose curl is a given vector field. This is analogous to a scalar potential, which is a scalar field whose negative gradient is a given vector field.

Formally, given a vector field v, a _____ is a vector field A such that

$$\mathbf{v} = \nabla \times \mathbf{A}.$$

If a vector field v admits a _____ A, then from the equality

$$\nabla \cdot (\nabla \times \mathbf{A}) = 0$$

(divergence of the curl is zero) one obtains

$$\nabla \cdot \mathbf{v} = \nabla \cdot (\nabla \times \mathbf{A}) = 0,$$

which implies that v must be a solenoidal vector field.

a. Moment of Inertia
b. Lagrangian
c. Wave equation
d. Vector potential

32. In physics, _____ is movement that changes the position of an object, as opposed to rotation. For example, according to Whittaker:

A _____ is the operation changing the positions of all points (x, y, z) of an object according to the formula

$$(x, y, z) \to (x + \Delta x, y + \Delta y, z + \Delta z)$$

where $(\Delta x, \Delta y, \Delta z)$ is the same vector for each point of the object. The _____ vector $(\Delta x, \Delta y, \Delta z)$ common to all points of the object describes a particular type of displacement of the object, usually called a linear displacement to distinguish it from displacements involving rotation, called angular displacements.

a. BIBO stability
b. BDDC
c. 15 theorem
d. Translation

33. The _____ is an important partial differential equation which describes the distribution of heat (or variation in temperature) in a given region over time. For a function u(x,y,z,t) of three spatial variables (x,y,z) and the time variable t, the _____ is

$$\frac{\partial u}{\partial t} - k\left(\frac{\partial^2 u}{\partial x^2} + \frac{\partial^2 u}{\partial y^2} + \frac{\partial^2 u}{\partial z^2}\right) = 0$$

or equivalently

$$\frac{\partial u}{\partial t} = k\nabla^2 u$$

where k is a constant.

The _____ is of fundamental importance in diverse scientific fields.

a. 15 theorem
b. Heat equation
c. BIBO stability
d. BDDC

Chapter 5. Surface Integrals and Vector Analysis

34. In mathematics a _____ is a construction in vector calculus which associates a vector to every point in a (locally) Euclidean space.

Vector fields are often used in physics to model, for example, the speed and direction of a moving fluid throughout space, or the strength and direction of some force, such as the magnetic or gravitational force, as it changes from point to point.

In the rigorous mathematical treatment, (tangent) vector fields are defined on manifolds as sections of a manifold's tangent bundle.

   a. BIBO stability
   b. 15 theorem
   c. BDDC
   d. Vector field

35. In geometry, the _____ is a particular mapping (function) that projects a sphere onto a plane. The projection is defined on the entire sphere, except at one point -- the projection point. Where it is defined, the mapping is smooth and bijective.
   a. 15 theorem
   b. BDDC
   c. Peirce quincuncial projection
   d. Stereographic projection

36. A _____ is a surface created by rotating a curve lying on some plane (the generatrix) around a straight line (the axis of rotation) that lies on the same plane.

Examples of surfaces generated by a straight line are the cylindrical and conical surfaces. A circle that is rotated about a (coplanar) axis through the center generates a sphere.

   a. Surface of revolution
   b. Riemann sum
   c. Shell integration
   d. Constant of integration

37. _____, S(x) and C(x), are two transcendental functions named after Augustin-Jean Fresnel that are used in optics. They arise in the description of near field Fresnel diffraction phenomena, and are defined through the following integral representations:

Chapter 5. Surface Integrals and Vector Analysis

$$S(x) = \int_0^x \sin(t^2)\, dt, \quad C(x) = \int_0^x \cos(t^2)\, dt.$$

The simultaneous parametric plot of S(x) and C(x) is the Cornu spiral, or clothoid.

Normalised _____, S(x) and C(x).

a. Differential
b. First derivative test
c. Leibniz function
d. Fresnel integrals

38. Just as the definite integral of a positive function of one variable represents the area of the region between the graph of the function and the x-axis, the _____ of a positive function of two variables represents the volume of the region between the surface defined by the function (on the three dimensional Cartesian plane where z = f(x,y)) and the plane which contains its domain. (Note that the same volume can be obtained via the triple integral -- the integral of a function in three variables -- of the constant function f(x, y, z) = 1 over the above-mentioned region between the surface and the plane.) If there are more variables, a multiple integral will yield hypervolumes of multi-dimensional functions.

a. Risch algorithm
b. Trigonometric substitution
c. Constant of integration
d. Double integral

39. A _____ is the portion of a solid--normally a cone or pyramid--which lies between two parallel planes cutting the solid. The term is commonly used in computer graphics to describe the 3d area which is visible on the screen (which is formed by a clipped pyramid.)

Each plane section is a base of the _____.

a. BIBO stability
b. BDDC
c. 15 theorem
d. Frustum

40. _____ is the name of several related measures of the size of an object, a surface, or an ensemble of points. It is calculated as the root mean square distance of the objects' parts from either its center of gravity or an axis.

In structural engineering, the two-dimensional _____ is used to describe the distribution of cross sectional area in a beam around its centroidal axis.

a. BIBO stability
b. BDDC
c. 15 theorem
d. Radius of gyration

41. The _____ specifies the relationship between the two central operations of calculus, differentiation and integration.

The first part of the theorem, sometimes called the first _____, shows that an indefinite integration can be reversed by a differentiation.

The second part, sometimes called the second _____, allows one to compute the definite integral of a function by using any one of its infinitely many antiderivatives.

a. Leibniz formula
b. Fundamental theorem of calculus
c. Periodic function
d. Limits of integration

Chapter 6. Vector Analysis in Higher Dimensions

1. A _____ officer is an officer of high military rank. The term or equivalent is used by nearly every country in the world. _____ can be used as a generic term for all grades of _____ officer, or it can specifically refer to a single rank that is just called _____.
    a. BDDC
    b. 15 theorem
    c. BIBO stability
    d. General

2. In elementary mathematics, physics, and engineering, a _____ is a geometric object that has both a magnitude (or length), direction and sense, (i.e., orientation along the given direction.) A _____ is frequently represented by a line segment with a definite direction, or graphically as an arrow, connecting an initial point A with a terminal point B, and denoted by

   ⟶

   The magnitude of the _____ is the length of the segment and the direction characterizes the displacement of B relative to A: how much one should move the point A to 'carry' it to the point B.

   Many algebraic operations on real numbers have close analogues for vectors.

    a. 15 theorem
    b. BDDC
    c. Linear partial differential operator
    d. Vector

3. In linear algebra, the null vector or _____ is the vector (0, 0, …, 0) in Euclidean space, all of whose components are zero. It is usually written $\vec{0}$ or 0 or simply 0. A _____ has no direction.
    a. Zero vector
    b. Direction vector
    c. Homogeneous function
    d. Scalar multiplication

4. In vector calculus, the _____ is shorthand for either the _____ matrix or its determinant, the _____ determinant.

   In algebraic geometry the _____ of a curve means the _____ variety: a group variety associated to the curve, in which the curve can be embedded.

   These concepts are all named after the mathematician Carl Gustav Jacob Jacobi.

Chapter 6. Vector Analysis in Higher Dimensions

a. Vector Laplacian
b. Saddle surface
c. Critical point
d. Jacobian

5. In infinitesimal calculus, a _____ is traditionally an infinitesimally small change in a variable. For example, if x is a variable, then a change in the value of x is often denoted Δx (or δx when this change is considered to be small.) The _____ dx represents such a change, but is infinitely small.

a. The Method of Mechanical Theorems
b. Dirichlet integral
c. Local maximum
d. Differential

6. In the mathematical fields of differential geometry and tensor calculus, differential forms are an approach to multivariable calculus that is independent of coordinates. A _____ of degree k, or (differential) k-form, on a smooth manifold M is a smooth section of the kth exterior power of the cotangent bundle of M. The set of all k-forms on M is a vector space commonly denoted $\Omega^k(M)$.

A differential 0-form is by definition a smooth function on M. A differential 1-form is an object dual to a vector field on M.

a. Hodge dual
b. Soldering
c. Two-form
d. Differential form

7. In economics, the _____ functional form of production functions is widely used to represent the relationship of an output to inputs. It was proposed by Knut Wicksell (1851-1926), and tested against statistical evidence by Charles Cobb and Paul Douglas in 1900-1928.

For production, the function is

$Y = AL^\alpha K^\beta$,

Chapter 6. Vector Analysis in Higher Dimensions

where:

- Y = total production (the monetary value of all goods produced in a year)
- L = labor input
- K = capital input
- A = total factor productivity
- α and β are the output elasticities of labor and capital, respectively. These values are constants determined by available technology.

Output elasticity measures the responsiveness of output to a change in levels of either labor or capital used in production, ceteris paribus. For example if α = 0.15, a 1% increase in labor would lead to approximately a 0.15% increase in output.

a. 15 theorem
b. BDDC
c. BIBO stability
d. Cobb-Douglas

8. In mathematics and its applications, a _____ system is a system for assigning an n-tuple of numbers or scalars to each point in an n-dimensional space. This concept is part of the theory of manifolds. 'Scalars' in many cases means real numbers, but, depending on context, can mean complex numbers or elements of some other commutative ring.
    a. Spherical coordinate system
    b. 15 theorem
    c. Coordinate
    d. Cylindrical coordinate system

9. In mathematics, a (topological) _____ is defined as follows: let I be an interval of real numbers (i.e. a non-empty connected subset of $\mathbb{R}$); then a _____ γ is a continuous mapping $\gamma : I \to X$, where X is a topological space. The _____ γ is said to be simple if it is injective, i.e. if for all x, y in I, we have $\gamma(x) = \gamma(y) \implies x = y$. If I is a closed bounded interval $[a, b]$, we also allow the possibility $\gamma(a) = \gamma(b)$ (this convention makes it possible to talk about closed simple _____.)
    a. Tractrix
    b. Curve
    c. Closed curve
    d. Prolate cycloid

10. In mathematics, _____ are a concept central to linear algebra and related fields of mathematics

Chapter 6. Vector Analysis in Higher Dimensions

Suppose that K is a field and V is a vector space over K. As usual, we call elements of V vectors and call elements of K scalars.

a. Fundamental theorem of algebra
b. Linear combinations
c. Permutation
d. 15 theorem

11. A surface S in the Euclidean space R^3 is _____ if a two-dimensional figure (for example,) cannot be moved around the surface and back to where it started so that it looks like its own mirror image (.) Otherwise the surface is non-_____.

More precisely, and applicable to non-embedded surfaces, a surface is non-_____ if there is a continuous map f from the product of a 2-dimensional disk D and the unit interval [0,1] to the surface, $f : D \times [0, 1] \to S$ such that f(c,t) = f(d,t) only if c = d for every t in [0,1], and there exists a reflection map r such that f(d,0) = f(r(d),1) for every d in D.

a. AUSM
b. ACTRAN
c. ALGOR
d. Orientable

12. In mathematics, an _____ on a real vector space is a choice of which ordered bases are 'positively' oriented and which are 'negatively' oriented. In the three-dimensional Euclidean space, the two possible basis orientations are called right-handed and left-handed (or right-chiral and left-chiral), respectively. However, the choice of _____ is independent of the handedness or chirality of the bases (although right-handed bases are typically declared to be positively oriented, they may also be assigned a negative _____.)

a. ACTRAN
b. ALGOR
c. Unit vector
d. Orientation

13. For an orientable surface, a consistent choice of 'clockwise' (as opposed to counter-clockwise) is called an orientation, and the surface is called _____. An orientable surface admits exactly 2 orientations, and the distinction between an _____ surface and an orientable surface is subtle and frequently blurred. An orientable surface is an abstract surface that admits an orientation, while an _____ surface is a surface that is abstractly orientable, and has the additional datum of a choice of one of the 2 possible orientations.

a. ALGOR
b. Oriented
c. AUSM
d. ACTRAN

14. In calculus, a branch of mathematics, the _____ is a measurement of how a function changes when its input changes. Loosely speaking, a _____ can be thought of as how much a quantity is changing at some given point. For example, the _____ of the position (or distance) of a vehicle with respect to time is the instantaneous velocity (respectively, instantaneous speed) at which the vehicle is traveling.

The process of finding a _____ is called differentiation. The fundamental theorem of calculus states that differentiation is the reverse process to integration.

a. Bounded function
b. Semi-differentiability
c. Stationary phase approximation
d. Derivative

15. In differential geometry, the _____ extends the concept of the differential of a function, which is a form of degree zero, to differential forms of higher degree. Its current form was invented by Élie Cartan.

The _____ d has the property that $d^2 = 0$ and is the differential (coboundary) used to define de Rham (and Alexander-Spanier) cohomology on forms.

a. ACTRAN
b. ALGOR
c. Exterior derivative
d. AUSM

16. In mathematics, an _____ space is a topological space whose dimension is n (where n is a fixed natural number.) The archetypical example is _____ Euclidean space, which describes Euclidean geometry in n dimensions.

Many familiar geometric objects can be generalized to any number of dimensions.

a. BIBO stability
b. BDDC
c. 15 theorem
d. N-dimensional

17. The _____ of any solid, liquid, plasma, vacuum or theoretical object is how much three-dimensional space it occupies, often quantified numerically. One-dimensional figures (such as lines) and two-dimensional shapes (such as squares) are assigned zero _____ in the three-dimensional space. _____ is commonly presented in units such as mL or cm^3 (milliliters or cubic centimeters.)

   a. Vector potential
   b. Dirac equation
   c. Volume
   d. Klein-Gordon equation

18. In calculus, and more generally in mathematical analysis, _____ is a rule that transforms the integral of products of functions into other, hopefully simpler, integrals. The rule arises from the product rule of differentiation.

If u = f(x), v = g(x), and the differentials du = f '(x) dx and dv = g'(x) dx; then in its simplest form the product rule is:

$$\int u\,dv = uv - \int v\,du.$$

Suppose f(x) and g(x) are two continuously differentiable functions.

   a. Integrand
   b. Arc length
   c. Integration by parametric derivatives
   d. Integration by parts

ANSWER KEY

Chapter 1
1. a	2. d	3. b	4. d	5. d	6. c	7. c	8. d	9. d	10. d
11. b	12. d	13. d	14. d	15. d	16. a	17. b	18. d	19. d	20. d
21. d	22. d	23. d	24. d	25. b	26. d	27. b	28. d	29. d	30. b
31. a	32. a	33. d	34. a	35. a	36. c	37. c			

Chapter 2
1. d	2. b	3. c	4. d	5. d	6. a	7. b	8. c	9. b	10. b
11. b	12. a	13. d	14. b	15. c	16. a	17. d	18. b	19. c	20. d
21. c	22. c	23. a	24. d	25. d	26. d	27. a	28. d	29. d	30. d
31. c	32. d	33. b	34. a	35. d	36. d	37. d	38. d	39. a	40. c
41. b	42. b	43. b	44. c	45. a	46. d	47. a	48. c	49. d	50. a
51. b	52. d	53. b	54. d	55. b	56. b	57. a	58. c	59. c	60. b
61. b	62. a	63. d	64. b	65. b	66. b	67. d	68. d	69. d	70. d
71. d	72. d	73. d	74. c	75. d	76. c	77. d	78. a	79. c	80. d
81. d	82. d	83. d	84. d	85. b	86. c	87. c	88. c	89. a	90. b
91. b	92. d	93. a	94. d	95. c	96. d	97. d	98. a	99. b	100. a
101. d	102. d	103. a							

Chapter 3
1. d	2. d	3. b	4. d	5. d	6. b	7. b	8. b	9. d	10. c
11. b	12. b	13. c	14. c	15. d	16. d	17. d	18. b	19. d	20. b
21. c	22. d	23. b	24. c	25. c	26. b	27. d	28. a	29. d	

Chapter 4
1. b	2. c	3. d	4. d	5. d	6. d	7. d	8. d	9. d	10. d
11. a	12. c	13. d	14. c	15. a	16. b	17. a	18. d	19. c	20. d
21. c									

Chapter 5
1. d	2. b	3. d	4. d	5. d	6. d	7. a	8. d	9. d	10. b
11. d	12. a	13. b	14. c	15. d	16. b	17. c	18. d	19. b	20. d
21. a	22. d	23. d	24. a	25. d	26. b	27. d	28. d	29. b	30. d
31. d	32. d	33. b	34. d	35. d	36. a	37. d	38. d	39. d	40. d
41. b									

Chapter 6
1. d	2. d	3. a	4. d	5. d	6. d	7. d	8. c	9. b	10. b
11. d	12. d	13. b	14. d	15. c	16. d	17. c	18. d		

www.ingramcontent.com/pod-product-compliance
Lightning Source LLC
Chambersburg PA
CBHW081848230426
43669CB00018B/2864